In My Stride

Helen Skelton

In My Stride

Lessons learned through life and adventure

HEADLINE

First published in 2023 by
HEADLINE PUBLISHING GROUP

1

Cataloguing in Publication Data is available from the British Library

Hardback ISBN 978 1 0354 1063 7
Trade paperback ISBN 978 1 0354 1067 5

Typeset in Garamond 3 by CC Book Production

Printed and bound in Great Britain by Clays Ltd, Elcograf S.p.A.

HEADLINE PUBLISHING GROUP
An Hachette UK Company
Carmelite House
50 Victoria Embankment
London EC4Y 0DZ

www.headline.co.uk
www.hachette.co.uk

Ernie, Louise and Elsie. Thank you.

Contents

Contents

Prologue

Lake Days Are Good Days

Early mornings can be chaos: tired children, lost school bags, missing socks and a hyperactive toddler. My kids have never been good sleepers and the boys, Ernie and Louis, always end up in my bed along with their wriggling little sister, Elsie. I often compare night-time at my house to a game of whack-a-mole, constant problems cropping up that I need to deal with at lightning speed. By first light, baby Elsie (as I suspect she will eternally be known) is awake, all wild hair and nonsense chat, so I extricate us both from the tangle of limbs and tiptoe downstairs, past the landing window which looks out over the garden. We always stop to see what sort of day it is. I tell Elsie to 'wave to the birdies' and an enthusiastic little hand goes up in greeting accompanied by her trademark 'Hiya!', which she will shout enthusiastically to everyone and everything. Very cute, although not always appropriate.

The first thing I do is put the kettle on and make myself a coffee in the massive mug I bought in Berlin when I was covering the World Swimming Championships. I prefer it to all the smart crockery I used to use, which is now gathering dust in the cupboard. I need a robust workhorse of a mug to get me through the bedlam of breakfast. Three small children to get dressed, fed and out of the door in time for school and nursery – what could possibly go wrong?!

Ernie, my eight-year-old, is down next and raring to go. Like me, he has ants in his pants and wants to be out and active the moment he is up. In contrast, I always have to go and wake six-year-old Louis, who would sleep until midday if I let him. Every morning he asks if it is a school day and, five times a week, I respond with, 'Yes, babe, it is.' Although I put their uniforms out the night before, there is usually a drama over an item of clothing: the wrong pair of shorts, a missing shoe, socks that don't go quite high enough up the shin. How there can be an issue when it is the same outfit they wear every day, I will never know. While the boys get dressed, Elsie rushes around trying to high-five them or give big cuddles. My boys may get irritable with each other but they never get cross with their sister and I imagine how wonderful her life will be, growing up surrounded by so much big-brotherly love.

Breakfast has gone rogue. My kids have got into the habit of picnic plates, which started at my parents' house as a treat and has somehow become the norm. My mum gives them a 'treat tray' of snacks they can graze on – it's a mini buffet! Now treat trays have somehow extended to breakfast and, while I am not happy about it, I pick my battles and this is not one I want to have. So I give them a selection of fruit, toast and yoghurt while Elsie wanders about with a banana. Sometimes my dad will have popped around the night before to make a jug of pancake batter and leave it for me, ready for the morning, so all I have to do is heat the pan and get flipping. It's one of the many things about my dad that makes my heart full. He knows how to help without making a big old song and dance about it. He and Mum give their constant and quiet support in a million different ways.

I have always found the car seat wrestle a stressful one; the contortionist abilities of a toddler should never be underestimated. I'm lucky that the boys can cycle to school, with Elsie and I trying to keep up on foot. Rain or shine, the boys fly down the hill on their bikes and are there before they have even noticed the weather. Sometimes I cycle with Elsie on the back or put her in the pushchair. If Dad calls in on his way to work he will sit with her so I can whizz down with the boys. Elsie goes to nursery two days a week and trots in without a backward glance. I was worried about her going but she is so happy there.

Once a week, when everyone is where they should be, I don't go back to the house. I drive to Lake Ullswater, a place which has been my playground since I was young. When I moved back to Cumbria last year – after almost twenty years away – going to the lake grounded me in my new life and gave me another reason to be here. After the rush of getting everyone to school and before the day runs away with itself, I either meet a friend for a walk or I go out on the water on my paddleboard. I set aside an hour, longer if I can get away with it, and I forget about the laundry, empty fridge, messy house and pile of life/work admin that I will return to. I am not interested in going to the gym or an exercise class and will always find excuses to cancel, but I never talk myself out of heading to the lake. It ticks the physical and mental health boxes and acts as a welcome reset button. I think this is what is now known as 'blue health' or 'green therapy' and people cleverer than me are researching and writing about the benefits of both. I just know that after a day spent outside with my family in the fresh country air, I sleep better, eat better and my kids are better behaved. It's something that's always been important to me and my tribe.

Being on my paddleboard in the middle of the vast lake makes me feel small and insignificant in a good way. Nature tells me I can't be in control of everything. Out here, the elements are in charge, demanding I let go of all my jumbled thoughts and exist in the moment. I have my safety float with me so I can jump off the board for a swim or glide around, watching the clouds scud overhead and keeping an eye out for a peregrine falcon. My parents worry about me going by myself, but the solitude is exactly why I do it. It gives me the chance to be alone and makes me feel alive.

I find being on water really relaxing. It's one of the few places where I don't think about anything. Other than staying upright. All I am aware of is the direction of the wind, the water and the fells. Here, the weather is in charge and I am happy to relinquish control. It is the perfect antidote to the juggle of parenting, work and travel. I love being a mum and I love my job too. It's a career and a life I picked, crafted and adore, but it doesn't mean there aren't challenges as I bounce between BBC's Radio 5 and *Morning Live*, or from rugby coverage for ITV to Channel 5's *This Week on the Farm*. I wouldn't change a thing, so no complaints; I'm just acknowledging that it can be a lot to navigate. As a hard worker and people-pleaser, I get caught up in all the things others need from me, but protecting my time with the kids has been my priority since the eldest came along. I have got better at saying no to things if they will take me away from home for too long, and I have swapped FOMO (fear of missing out) for JOMO (joy of missing out), although it's still a work in progress. I am continually looking for balance, so staying upright on a wobbly board in moving water is a physical reminder of this.

There have been times in my life when I have forgotten about the power of the natural world and how important it is to be immersed in it. Every big adventure I have undertaken has reminded me all over again, whether it was kayaking down the Amazon, cycling to the South Pole or running an ultra-marathon in Namibia. I find it comforting to throw myself on nature's mercy and humbling to take on difficult tasks. I have always seen challenges as good training for life: the harder the challenge, the better prepared you are for what life may throw at you. It's not about battling the wildness, defeating it and standing proud at the top of a mountain with a fist raised. It's about journeying through the elements, blurring into the landscape and realising you have more in the tank than you thought. And wow, that is a confidence boost.

Life has a funny habit of throwing curveballs and it can be frustrating when we are told to be Confident! Resilient! Courageous! I don't know about you, but I have never been able to click my fingers and stop being afraid of something. What I do know is choosing to put myself in some gut-wrenchingly nerve-wracking situations has served me well, given me empathy and prepared me for things I would have preferred not to deal with. In these pages, I recount those times when I was pushed beyond my limits and how I discovered my confidence, resilience and courage through the adventures I undertook. There are secrets to share, lessons to learn, laughs to be had and ass to be kicked. Ready to dig deep with me?

1

Muddy Wellies and Microphones

*'Growing up on a farm has defined the person I am today.
Death and bad weather were part of my childhood and showed
me how little control we have in life.'*

Farming is in my DNA. It's what my dad did, his dad before
him and his before him. For years, Dad reminded me that lots
of daughters go into farming too. I dabbled but it wasn't for
me. I have no doubt Dad is chuffed to see how part of my telly
career is spent on farming shows. I would never describe myself
as a farmer but I think if it's the world you grow up in it shapes
you in ways you don't realise – rural life is under my fingernails
and caked on my muddy wellies. This is evident both when
I am working with farmers and with telly people.

I grew up on the family farm in Cumbria and, for the last five years, I have presented Channel 5's *This Week on the Farm,* a live seasonal series from Cannon Hall Farm in Yorkshire, just down the road from home. I am very proud of the programme we make, which gives viewers a real insight into what life is like in farming and celebrates the work of industrious local producers. It fascinates me how trendy farming has become. Local produce, fewer food miles, organic ethics and seasonal living are rules that govern the countryside, but they are now popular more widely and I am both buoyed and intrigued by farming's increasing popularity beyond rural communities.

Filming on a farm may not be the most glamorous gig in showbusiness. I always leave with shit on my shoes, usually smelling like a pig, and have been known to be elbow-deep inside an ewe while it's giving birth, but it's nowhere near as hard as actual farming. I love the way my two worlds collide. It's funny how life can come full circle.

Just like working on a farm, telly is all about teamwork and I am part of a fantastic group of presenters and production crew, but the real stars of the show are the animals. Like Jon Bon Pony, the Shetland with the mad fringe, and the goats Biscuit and Waffle, whom my kids begged me to bring home. My dad vetoed that, although I know he feels guilty for not giving my children a life surrounded by farm animals like I had. He shouldn't. Without the tie of a dairy herd, he is free to spend more time with his grandchildren and that is more precious. It's not something I would ever swap for a couple of goats.

We rarely stick to the television script because we need to be ready to respond to what is happening around us on the farm. As much as we want to make great telly, the livestock comes first and decisions are made regardless of the cameras. Who can say when a lamb will be born or whether it will need a helping hand to come into the world? It keeps me on my toes, which I love as a broadcaster and am used to as the daughter of a farmer. It's a natural adrenaline that's hard to find in domestic life. I may be in clean jeans with a full face of make-up and a blow dry, but I am still the feral child of my past getting stuck into the action where I can.

In one spring episode, we were filming with the calves, and I put my hand out to a bottle-fed calf who clamped its slobbering jaw around my hand and began to suckle. I didn't really think about it, but the bemused crew wanted to know why I didn't just pull my hand away. I was keeping the calf close while we filmed the scene, but the truth was I was also doing it for me. It was nostalgic to feel the raspy, sandpapery tongue of a little heifer and it transported me straight back to my childhood, growing up on a dairy farm. A reflex, I guess.

Years ago, I was filming at Chatsworth for another beloved rural programme, BBC's *Countryfile,* which I was part of for eight years. The set-up was taking some time (these things usually do) so I sat down cross-legged in a field looking out over the estate while the camera crew were up on a hill to get a wide shot. An enormous cow wandered over to me and I put my hand out in greeting. It had a good sniff and stood around for a bit before wandering off. I assumed the crew had got the shot so I walked back up the hill to them and when I got there they were speechless. They couldn't believe I had been sitting underneath an animal big enough to crush me and hadn't moved away. What if it had trampled me? Of course, I knew that wasn't going to happen because it was calm, cumbersome and content in its world and I wasn't bothering it, but I was surprised by their reaction. It was just second nature to me.

The owners of Cannon Hall, farming brothers Rob and Dave Nicholson, are also part of the Channel 5 presenting team. My childhood was identical to theirs and we share a cultural language which reminds me of home. We often do or say things without realising it that may look odd to people who weren't brought up on a farm. Like when we were waiting for the crew to set up and, while we chatted, we each picked a blade of grass. We touched the electric fence with it and gave ourselves a mild electric shock. The crew couldn't understand why on earth we would do this to ourselves. We just shrugged. It's what we did as farm kids, partly to check whether the fence was on and also for the thrill of the mild shock. My two sons, Ernie and Louis, were there and Rob jokingly told them about the times he and Dave used to pee on an electric fence and how the shock would travel straight up the stream of wee to their willies! Of course, my boys thought this was hilarious. We all insisted they never do it but that made the idea even more appealing to them. I overheard them telling a couple of school mates about their mum's pals who pee on electric fences and, funnily enough, they haven't been invited to their house for a play date.

A while ago, one of the farmers on the programme was talking about buying a house in Spain. Rob, Dave and I discussed how that would be received by non-farmers as opposed to farmers. Non-farmers would respond positively in the manner of, 'Wow, that's exciting, good for you!' Not farming folk. Oh no. Instead, we say, 'Who does he think he is, buying houses abroad? What's that all about, is he some sort of playboy?!' It's a classic farming response and the type of conversation we would have around the kitchen table at home. Or in the local social club. In the village near Cannon Hall Farm they have two social clubs, at the top and bottom of the hill, so one is called Top Club and the other is called Bottom Club. It's easy to make a decision about where to meet for a drink. When I lived in the city, I didn't realise how much I missed this sort of connection and simplicity.

We film the show in blocks – a week here, a week there – which makes it easier to fit around family life. I filmed one series when I was nine months pregnant with Elsie. By the following series she was a few months old and she came with me. I would escape to the sound truck to breastfeed her. I have known Mick, the sound man, for twenty years. I have sat in his van on the side of our makeshift TV set chatting to him about everything from sheep and children to relationships. I am very lucky that my kids can sometimes come to set with me and are used to being on a farm. They call our crew room, where everyone gets food and snacks, 'the shop where you don't pay' and they think it is wild that I can get a can of Coca-Cola for free at work. Do they care about me being on TV? Nope. They just care about the availability of snacks and sweets. Being at work with me is normal to them so they know how to behave respectfully and understand the dangers, both on a TV set and in a farmyard. That's quite some experience and I hope one day they will look back and think it was cool.

I always look forward to returning to Cannon Hall for a new series. In the beginning, I was surprised by the amount of attention the programme received. I wasn't sure how many people would want to watch a lamb being born, but it turns out quite a lot do. This can still catch me by surprise because when I was growing up only farmers were interested in farming and at school, their children (me) were considered old-fashioned, uncool and a bit smelly. Not so now. Thankfully, many more people are embracing nature, championing agriculture and growing their own.

My dad inherited the farm from his parents. I adored my grandparents and I was incredibly close to them. They were like gods to me. They were also a sitcom waiting to happen. My granny was very well-to-do and had grown up in a castle, whereas my grandad was an absolute scally who had already been engaged several times before he married her. His family history was full of estranged relatives who had gambled farms away, which was the opposite to my grandmother's tribe, who were pillars of the local community. Whatever the chemistry was between them, it worked. They lived in Ecclefechan on the Scottish Borders before moving to a farm near Penrith, where they brought their children up, one of whom was my dad. When Dad took over the farm, my grandparents moved to a cottage in the next village and I saw them every day. Grandad still came and pottered around the farm and most days when I got back from school, he would pop in for a cuppa and Rich Tea biscuits spread with butter and jam.

The farmhouse was a sanctuary for me then and it still is now. The front of the house looks out across the fells and the back of the house faces towards the Pennines. I can't think of two more glorious places to be sandwiched between. Me and my brother, Gavin – who is a couple of years older than me – had an idyllic Enid Blyton-style childhood, not that we realised how lucky we were back then. We didn't know any different. We had loads of space and would invite all our friends to come and hang out or camp in the garden. Every hour was spent outside, paddling in the river just over the hill, building rafts, getting mucky and climbing things I shouldn't have. I was definitely in trouble a lot more than my brother. Mum said in an interview she was persuaded to do when I was on *Strictly Come Dancing* that, 'Helen has always done things her own way.' This is a sentence that can be interpreted in many different ways but I am going to take it as an acknowledgement that I was independent at an early age! Like when I got a crew cut aged four. I had very long, sun-kissed hair and a boy I used to play with at school decided to take the garden shears to it, cutting it close to my scalp. I was thrilled! I can imagine some little girls would be devastated but I was really pleased with my short hair. Mum nearly passed out when she saw me.

When we played hide and seek, I would shimmy up the side of the barn and perch on the roof so my brother couldn't find me, until Dad caught me one day and took me to the local builder, who gave me a lecture about the risk of falling through the roof and the dangers of asbestos. I remember my parents always being around. Dad's office was in the farmyard next to the house so we could pop in and see him whenever we wanted. I would often help him with the milking too. A memory seared in my mind is the day one of the cows was ill. I could only have been about five. The cow had milk fever and had collapsed on the floor of the milking parlour, so we had to give her calcium through a drip. It was a dangerous process because as soon as the calcium hit the cow's system it acted like a shot of adrenaline and the hefty animal would start bouncing around. To keep me safe, Dad lifted me into the hay rack on the wall, which was six feet off the ground. From there I could hold the bottle of medicine while he administered it. I remember being really proud that I had helped Dad and made the cow better.

Our primary school was in the local village, surrounded by fields of sheep and cows. I went to the same school that my dad had attended, and I played with the kids of his friends. My bestie Amy's parents are best pals of my parents and now my daughter plays with her kids. We are just like family, albeit not in blood. I only hope my daughter and Amy's don't decapitate as many Barbies as we did. It was innocent if not macabre.

The school was a lovely place to be, and tiny, with just a few children in each year. Mum would drive us there as it was too far to walk. Our farm wasn't that remote but for a lot of my school friends it was a mission to get anywhere as it's quite a rural part of the world. At secondary school, if it rained a lot, we would get sent home because there was a danger the bridge would collapse and the old Second World War siren in the town would go off as a warning. We loved that sound because it signalled a swift retreat home. We also revelled in snowy days as school would close and we would head to the foot of the Pennines for sledging.

At school, I was known as Gavin's little sister. He was academic, very sporty, popular and an excellent football player (he played professionally in Scotland throughout his career and now coaches in League One), so he was a tough act to follow. If he had mates over I would try to join in, playing football or cricket with them if they let me. I suspect it will be the same for Elsie as my garden is usually full of her brothers and their friends. She loves it and bangs on the door to join them. She has chased them with a football from the minute she could walk. She has a pram and a dolly but I guess she copies what she sees. Dad bought her a toy hoover and chainsaw from the charity shop because he said he didn't want to stereotype her. You may be a white Cumbrian dairy farmer, Dad, but you're also a feminist. As he's proved on national telly, but that's for later in the book.

I suppose Elsie has no choice whether she likes football or not because my entire family is football mad. Back in the day, we would think nothing of travelling around the country to attend weekend matches. We used to have Sunday dinner on a Saturday because my brother played football on a Sunday, so until I was fifteen, I thought it was traditional to eat a roast on a Saturday. I didn't care which day I ate it as long as we had it! I also didn't care about hours in the car traversing the country, listening to sports reports and eating fish and chips. I'll never forget my parents taking us to watch Luton versus Carlisle United. Luton is perhaps the polar opposite to the part of the world I knew. We shuffled through the terraced houses that double up as turnstiles for the football and I took it all in. So many different people united by a deep love and appreciation of a sport. I didn't realise it then but I appreciate this now, and football, for all the criticism levelled at it, showed me life beyond the Pennines.

The farmhouse kitchen was the heart of the home. There was always something going on and people were in and out all day. My absolute favourite part of the year was silage time, which began in late spring and continued until the end of the summer. It was when the grass would be cut and brought into the barns to store for winter feed for the animals. I thought it was the most exciting event, with around six contractors working long days, racing against the weather and light. We would make piles of sandwiches and take them out to the workers. Dad would send Gavin and me into the middle of the field to lay down in the grass and, if he could still see us, it meant the grass wasn't long enough to cut. I felt important and integral to the operation.

Now that I have my own kids I am forever asking myself if they're shaped more by nurture or nature. Are mine wild because of the way I bring them up or is it who they are? I look back at my own experiences growing up and, while my mum does not share my adventurous spirit – she hates lifts and I made a living jumping out of planes – I definitely get a lot of other qualities from her. Many daughters hate to admit that they are turning into their mothers but I know I am, and not just because comfortable shoes from Marks & Spencer are looking increasingly attractive. I can see a fire in her belly that perhaps I had never appreciated. At times, I have wrongly assumed that she was without drive or ambition. But maybe I have been the foolish one, chasing after a life other than the already wonderful one right here on my doorstep. I should give her more credit for crafting a quality of life and a relationship with her children that has created the most amazing family.

So, no, Mum would never jump out of a plane but she's a lion when it comes to getting her kids on their feet – and other people's kids, too, as a pre-school teacher. From a very early age, I saw her do things with gumption; she never did things half-heartedly, even when it meant holding her nerve enough to get on my skateboard. If we were doing fancy dress she would make a whole scene, like the time I was Alice in Wonderland; my brother was a hare and we had a cart with other Wonderland animals on. She always says, 'You only get out of life what you put in.' I hope some of her maternal spirit has rubbed off on me. She came to every school play and sports fixture and was always an encouraging presence, never pushy.

Not only did she look after us all and help Dad on the farm, but when we were teenagers, in the run up to Christmas, she would work in a factory to earn extra money. She hated the job but she did it so they could afford to buy us presents. Of course, she doesn't see it like that, she just did stuff without making a fuss, but I can see now how she put us first and still does to this day. This has made a lasting impression on me and it's how I parent my own kids.

Dad rarely took a day off and was up at 5am every morning to head out to the dairy. Christmas Day was no different. We would be allowed to open one gift during the agonising wait for his return. When he came in he would then have to shower so our patience was stretched to its absolute limit! You can imagine how much it took to get him to have a week's holiday. When I was doing *Countryfile,* I once joked around with a farmer because he had a passport. Fancy that! In fairness, Dad had one too and we would spend our precious week somewhere lovely like Menorca or Ibiza. Anywhere with a beach, basically. I was very conscious that an aunt and uncle travelled a lot and worked abroad, which I always thought was so exotic. We may not have had that sort of upbringing but because we lived in an isolated rural community, my parents made sure we got out as much as possible. Mum would take me to Manchester to go shopping and see a show, and to this day I am happy to travel long distances because if I didn't, I would never leave Cumbria!

My brother Gavin and I both have a really strong work ethic, which comes from our parents. In fact, I think he works too hard, but he would probably say the same about me. Sometimes I am asked to do something that may not fit logistically with the kids so I wrestle with the decision, but it is very simple for Dad. He always says I should do it because they will pay me and isn't that the point of having a job? This is then swiftly followed by him and Mum offering to help with the kids so I can take the opportunity. I adore my stoic but sensitive Dad. You won't find anyone who can say a bad word about him.

As well as having a great brother, I have a gang of lovely cousins. My mum has three brothers and they each had two daughters, so I was surrounded by female cousins from birth. When I was growing up, being the second youngest was difficult and I could feel a bit henpecked. It was impossible to have a secret or get away with anything as Mum always found out. But now it feels like I have an army of fantastic sisters.

I began to get restless as I got older. My favourite TV programmes were *Byker Grove* and *Grange Hill*, which were set in worlds that couldn't have been more different from the life I led. I was longing for a youth club to head to on a Friday night. Suddenly, life away from the farm began to look more appealing. I didn't appreciate the freedom I had and the environment I was immersed in until I moved away. When I was married and lived in Leeds, I really missed the Lakes. I would just want to be near water on a hot day, so I would take the kids to the local park and put them in the river. I know some people thought it was a bit gross but it was what I was used to.

I can see how growing up on a farm has defined the person I am today. Death and bad weather were part of my childhood and showed me how little control we have in life. I think this gave me the ability to accept the things I couldn't change and showed me how to deal with hard emotions. I am OK with the unknown. I would go as far as to say I welcome it. I think these are the most valuable lessons I learned in my childhood. That, and the importance of family, which is something I have continued to rely on throughout my life, now more than ever.

2

Teenage Ambition

'When the cards of life deal me one that hurts, my reaction is to take on something difficult, perhaps to distract myself by doing something I perceive to be more painful.'

'Is it as tough as it looks?' This is the question everyone asks if Channel 4's *Celebrity SAS: Who Dares Wins* is mentioned. 'No, it's tougher,' I always reply. Not because of the physical challenges – I actually enjoyed many of them – but because the anxiety-inducing rants, lack of sleep and constant teasing that you might be thrown out of a helicopter or have to box one of your teammates are beyond stressful. So stressful, in fact, that we resorted to using a bucket in the corner of the bedroom as an emergency toilet because we didn't think we would have time to get to the loo block before we were summoned again. Trust me, seeing some of my class of *SAS* do a number two in the corner is not something you can unsee.

For me, the mind games were the hardest to deal with. I'd had a few things to contend with in my personal life and I wanted to escape reality by jumping into an immersive show. When the cards of life deal me one that hurts, my reaction is to take on something difficult, perhaps to distract myself by doing something I perceive to be more painful. It's a pattern I can recognise as I get older.

Maybe a juice retreat would have been a better idea but I had the opportunity to do *SAS* and I thought this could be the ultimate, all-consuming challenge, extreme enough to swallow me up. I underestimated the interrogations, where buttons are pushed and emotions explored. The contestants are hooded with wrists bound and led to a secret bunker where they are questioned relentlessly in the hope that the SAS guys can expose a chink in their armour. I thought I was prepared for this. They knew I didn't have much to hide in terms of my childhood or past trauma, and I tucked away anything that could be seen as weakness. I put up what I thought was an impenetrable mental barricade. Ha!

After a brusque preamble, SAS interrogator Ant Middleton went for the jugular. He said they thought I was the sort of girl at school who would wind boys up and pitch them against each other until they fought. This was not the sort of intimidation I was ready for and it completely blindsided me. They had found an Achilles heel I didn't even realise existed. As they were hauling me over the verbal coals, accusing me of flirting my way through my teen years and manipulating boys, I thought, *What if they are right? What if I did do that?* I used to have a boyfriend who was always getting into fights. I hadn't thought it was anything to do with me, but what if it was? I can't tell you how much of a curve ball that was for me. Admittedly, I was on the edge already, surviving on little sleep, limited food and missing my family. Of course, this was exactly what the *SAS* team had set out to do, they were very clever, but I don't think even they realised the impact they had. It was nothing compared to other contestants' opening up about grief, mental issues or difficult childhoods, but it bloody hurt. Imagine someone taunting you about the worst thing you think about yourself. They pushed buttons I didn't know I had and it made me think hard about my teen years.

I was probably a bit of a pain in the arse at my old-fashioned grammar secondary school. I may have been in the top set for most subjects and part of the sport teams, but on reflection I suspect I was also cheeky. Teachers would moan at me for asking too many questions and I would say, 'Surely that's what you want from your students?!' This backchat didn't go down too well. When I went into sixth form, I put myself forward for the position of head girl. The students and some of the teachers voted for me, but the headmaster was not on board. Eventually, he did relent and I took on the role, which, for me, was all about organising the end of year party.

Dad was always trying to get me to join the Young Farmer's Club and I resisted, maybe because the farming set at school weren't the cool kids. Instead, my social life was led by boys in my class, who used to hire village halls and do DJ sets. They would bring their decks and we would bring bottles of Martini or Malibu. There were flirtations but nothing serious because we were all too interested in partying as a group. Maybe I am remembering this through rose-tinted glasses, but there weren't many big teen dramas and we didn't tend to argue or fight over boys. In chemistry class every Wednesday, we would sit at the back and work out which tracksuit top and flared jean combo we were going to wear that weekend. We saved our Adidas Gazelles for Friday night when we danced to loud music in village halls in rural Cumbria. From here, we quickly progressed to Saturday nights spent at Brough club, a truck stop by day which transformed to a nightclub in the evening.

As we got older, our social scene stretched to Tall Trees, a nightclub in Yarm where you could get thrown into the swimming pool, and then beyond, to Newcastle. It was the mid-to-late nineties and even rural Cumbrian kids knew about drugs, but I never touched them. I think this was partly due to the legacy of Leah Betts, the eighteen-year-old who tragically died after taking ecstasy. I still remember her heartbroken parents talking about their loss. There was also a hard-hitting storyline in *Byker Grove* and a promise I made to my Dad. Seeing the effects drugs had on people really scared me. Maybe I am just a square. Even as an independent teenager I wanted to hold good the vow I'd made to my dad to stay away from ecstasy, ketamine and whatever else might be passed around in dark corners.

My parents always came out to pick me up regardless of the hour, driving down dark, winding country lanes in the middle of the night. They were right to be scared of what could happen. My community is not immune to the loss of teenage life. It would be wrong of me to talk about someone else's tragedy, but I have seen first-hand how hard it is for young people to lose one of their own and how, in a close-knit community, the ripples of tragedy affect so many in different ways.

The girls I hung out with then are the girls I still hang out with today. Only now, our Wednesday chat is dominated by whose kids will be at cricket on Friday night and whether we can have wine together while they play. At school and to this day, Kim has always been an instigator, an organiser and a source of great fun. Jill, Olga, Shellie, Rebecca and Holly were our core gang. If we were going out in Penrith we would get ready at my house. We would get ready at Kim's if we were heading to Brough, given that she lived on a caravan park with an outdoor swimming pool, we sometimes ended the night with a 2am dip. There was a campsite there as well as lodges and static caravans, with families from Middlesborough and Newcastle staying there. We thought these kids were so exotic! I worked in the takeaway on the site and finished my shift with a pocket full of five-pound tips, but stinking like a deep-fat fryer. When I wasn't smelling of chips I would often have a whiff of the dairy cow about me, as Dad would pay me to help muck out occasionally. On reflection, it's not hard to see why I was single.

I hated primary school. I cried every day for the first year and had to be peeled away from Mum, and it took me time to find my feet at secondary school too. I carried a lot of puppy fat and was one of the youngest in the year, but I blossomed in time for sixth form and finally started enjoying school. I worked hard on French, psychology and history A levels, with the occasional midweek bunk-off to go to the tarn with my mates to swim. There was pressure from school to go to university and I was offered a place at Durham to study Japanese, which I know is a bit random but how else was I going to get to Japan?! That was my sole reason for choosing the degree, which was probably a bit daft.

*   *   *

The summer, straight after A levels, I went on a girls' holiday. I wasn't yet eighteen so I had to take a note of agreement from my parents to the travel agent. We had a blast and this led to a second trip with a one-way EasyJet ticket to Nice with my friend Jill. Inspired by my cousins, who had worked in bars in Greece and returned with amazing tales of wild times, I wanted a summer of adventure and to throw myself into a new challenge. I was at a crossroads in my life. Everyone around me was excited about university and I wasn't. So off Jill and I went, a couple of naïve teenagers with heavy backpacks, nowhere to stay and no job, to a French town where millionaires go to play. European backpackers tend to congregate, and we bumped into people who pointed us in the direction of places to stay and get work. We found an apartment and rented it for the summer. This was before the days of Airbnb and Booking.com, so convincing French estate agents to rent us a flat wasn't easy, but somehow we managed it. Plenty went wrong and plenty went right. We got jobs, we lost jobs, we felt out of our depth and then we hit our stride.

When I look back and think of the way we were spoken to by the French restaurant owners who employed us, it wasn't good. The waiters were just as harsh and rude to us, but my French wasn't amazing so ignorance was bliss. I was a wide-eyed seventeen-year-old blonde who was having the time of her life. We slept on the beach during the day, cleared dishes from tables in crowded tourist restaurants in the evening and partied all night. We met other teenagers from what felt like every European city and hung out with Australian boys working on expensive yachts. It was a rite of passage, an eye-opener and a trip which Jill and I will still laugh about when we are ninety. Oh, the summer we survived on Nutella crêpes bought from street vendors at 4am and had flirty banter with tanned boys who cleaned boats!

We returned home a couple of months later. Jill was keen to get her exam results; me, not so much as I still wasn't sure what I was going to do next. We both did really well in our exams and Jill skipped off to Oxford to study law. I have always been super proud of her and her achievements. I know you would like her if you met her, everyone does. She is the expert juggler of a lovely family and a successful career as a top lawyer in a big firm and is a shining example for women like me who are trying to balance work and kids. Despite her ridiculous schedule, Jill still finds time to help others and support projects she is passionate about. It's not relevant here but I could write a chapter about each of my closest friends, to share how instrumental they are in my life and the joy they bring.

Despite me getting good results, I pulled out of university. Yep, that's right. I had the clear and certain realisation that it wasn't for me. I think I had always known this but I'd thought I had to follow the traditional path. One taste of freedom and

I was hooked, so I broke it to my parents. It went a bit like this . . .

Parents, calmly: OK, Helen, so if you aren't going to accept the university place you worked so hard for, what are you going to do?

Me, dreamily: Well, I want to go travelling and I want to be like the Australians on the yachts and ping-pong around the world.

Parents, deadpan: And how are you going to pay for that?

Fair point.

After their sensible intervention, I took a more practical view as to what was next. I enrolled on a journalism course at Carlisle College and looked for appropriate work experience, getting a Saturday job in the newsroom at local radio station CFM. One weekend, I went to watch my brother play football and I got chatting to one of the sport reporters. I said I would quite like to do his job, so he invited me to shadow him and arranged for me to do work experience at BBC Radio Cumbria. I answered the phones, delivered faxes (remember those?!) and recorded vox pops for them. I was up for anything that kept me learning and made me useful. I had been taught how to edit at college and was excited by the modern technology that irritated my older colleagues. They didn't want anything to change. They also said, 'Helen, what you've got to understand is, you will not get a job at the BBC until you get a post grad in journalism.' And yet, when university students would come in for work experience, they couldn't pronounce some of the place names, they didn't have any local contacts and they couldn't get story leads. Unlike me, the local lass. I would go into the meetings where we were all supposed to pitch stories and I was often the only person to put my hand up. Gavin played football locally, Mum worked in a school and Dad was a well-respected dairy farmer, so I knew about proposed road plans, player transfers and schools going into special measures. I am not saying I was any better than the university kids but I was well connected and hungry for it, I learned quickly and I could talk to people. Ultimately, that's what it's about.

At college, I saw a poster on the noticeboard from Border Television, who were looking for someone to read out birthday cards once a week after the regional news. I auditioned and got the job! In hindsight, I may have been the only one who went for it, but a win is a win, right? And it put me exactly where I needed to be, at the heart of a small but successful regional TV station. Now I had new lessons to learn. It was never about being a presenter; I didn't care about being on screen. It was about what it took to get a programme on the air, from the newsroom to the camera operator to the gallery. This was exactly what I wanted to do with my life so I volunteered for everything and they let me get involved.

Times were changing and jobs were merging so I could be in front of the camera, behind it or both. I wasn't bothered. I just wanted to be in the TV world. It was regional television, with plenty of quirks and characters, but mainly full of wonderful people who loved what they did. One colleague, Livy Ellis, made me realise early on that television is so rarely about the person in front of the camera. There is an army of people making it work and every cog in that wheel counts. Two of the best, with whom I have stayed in contact over the years, were the local celebrity newsreaders, husband-and-wife team Susanna Boccaccio and John Hawkins. They took me under their encouraging and supportive wings. I have a lot to thank them for. To this day, when I think about those people and that time, I can smell the canteen, I can feel the wiry carpet under my feet and I still smirk about the big-shot London TV presenter who came in one week to record a programme and kept sending the runner out to buy her tampons. I have no idea if it was a trick or a power trip, but it was another early lesson in what's appropriate and what leaves an impression on a production team.

So there I was, my life split four joyous ways, between college, my radio job, the TV station and my much older boyfriend.

My parents had balked at the eight-year age gap at first but they saw I was happy with him. When I finished college, I was exhausted by the combination of studying and working on local news at the weekends. Seduced by the idea of a low-adrenaline, Monday-to-Friday, nine-to-five life with free weekends, I got a job at a local PR company. I was terrible at it. I had to suck up to rich hotel clients who were paying lots of money and go out for fancy dinners on work credit cards. In theory, it was a plum opportunity for a twenty-one-year old and my PR colleagues were great, but in practice, I just couldn't do it. I couldn't be fake. The posh menus couldn't swing it; I would rather eat my own feet.

Throughout this time, I had kept my hand in at BBC Radio Cumbria, so I asked for more freelance shifts. I took anything that was available.

You need me to get up at 4am? No problem.

You want me to stand outside a courtroom till midnight? No problem.

You need me to sit in the county council meeting for four hours of mind-numbing debate on the unlikely off-chance there may be a story, though there never is? ABSOLUTELY NO PROBLEM.

I remember driving to Newcastle before sunrise one day to sit in a radio car in a layby to do a quick radio piece. Just before I was due on air, they told me they weren't coming to me because they had run out of time. 'No problem,' I said. And it really wasn't. I didn't care as long as I was part of the team.

Then something radical happened. I was offered the breakfast show on BBC Radio Cumbria. I couldn't believe it! At twenty-two, I was the youngest presenter on the flagship radio show, broadcasting alongside a Radio Cumbria stalwart, who I was hoping would be an inspiring mentor. It was a challenging environment and after each show I would go into the debrief meeting and my mentor would disappear. He probably didn't like me very much. After a year, the bosses made the decision to take the show off air and I returned to the newsroom. Not only was I back where I'd started but my relationship had just broken up too.

My boyfriend had a quick temper and would often get into fights. At the time, I didn't think it was anything to do with me. He was the one with anger management problems. And yet, however many years later, there I was in a dark room being confronted by the *Celebrity SAS* gang, who were suggesting the exact opposite. Was it my fault that he would get cross and fight? No, it was not. I was never even there when it happened. But in that strange interrogation atmosphere, I wasn't sure.

We can often feel accountable for the actions of those close to us when they should be taking responsibility for their own behaviour. Over the years, I know I have made excuses for other people, giving them the benefit of the doubt or assuming it was something I said or did that had caused them to react. This set a precedent in the way they then treated me, which isn't great. It can be hard to step out of a situation and look at it objectively. Being slammed by the SAS guys stirred up feelings I didn't recognise, but now that I've had time to consider it, I think they were wrong. I was not that girl. I didn't provoke boys or try to play them off against each other, and my boyfriend's behaviour was not a reflection on me either. I will always be the person who sees the wider context of a situation and takes all the factors into account.

I found myself at an important crossroads, although to be fair there wasn't much of a choice to make. I had caught my boyfriend flirting with someone else, which created an awful lot of drama at the time and finally ended our flagging relationship. My first experience of heartbreak was agony. I remember thinking it hurt to breathe and that nothing else in my life would ever be as bad. Bless my cotton socks.

As well as that, my flagship show was over and, with it, my career – before it had even got going – so I really didn't have much more to gamble with. Up until this point, everything I had done had a momentum to it and I'd felt I was getting somewhere, even though I wasn't sure where I wanted to be. Now I was stuck and only I could get myself out of it. Still, deciding to change my life took a level of bravery I had not known I possessed and it set the tone for what was to come.

3

Bright Lights, Big City

'You had to know who you were, what you wanted
and where you were heading, and I was still trying
to work it all out. It showed.'

I got my arse out of Cumbria and went looking for adventure. I went to London.

When I arrived, I had no job and sofa-surfed at friends' houses for a few weeks. My friend Jill, who I had been to France with, let me share her bed in Islington and I will never forget her paying for my taxi from the train station to her house. It was a small act of kindness that will always stay with me, just as touching as her arriving, many years later, armed with ice lollies in the midst of my marriage break-up. Another of our gang, Rebecca, let me sleep on her couch in Camden. We were born in the same hospital within days of each other, a few beds apart. Two decades on, we were finding our feet together in London. Albeit her with a good degree and a sensible head on her shoulders, and me with no plan, no prospects and too embarrassed to return home. Percy Pigs always remind me of this time because Rebecca's flatmate worked for Marks & Spencer and he would bring home samples. For a few months, I think I mostly survived on sweets. My old life was over and my new life was about to begin.

I tapped up any contact I had, however vague, and asked if they knew of work, which got me a few shifts at Sky Sports News because of my apparent knowledge of lower-league Scottish football. Unbeknownst to them, I was just regurgitating information I had picked up from watching my brother play football and dating an ex-teammate of his. The snippets I'd overheard in my social circle proved enough to get me over the threshold and earned me a few shifts in production. I was a dab hand at cutting goals and writing reports of who beat who on a rainy Tuesday night in Inverness. It was like nothing I had experienced before. I loved it and thrived on being surrounded by people who also loved what they did. However, a lot of the women there wanted to be on screen, so it was incredibly competitive. They had paid their dues in the office and they didn't want anyone jumping the queue, so I was eyed suspiciously.

I didn't fit in. You had to know who you were, what you wanted and where you were heading, and I was still trying to work it all out. It showed.

I am not sure it was fun, but it was a learning curve and it did open up an opportunity for me on BBC's *Sportsround,* where I met Jake Humphrey. He was an absolute dream to work with and became a good pal, showing me the ropes in those early weeks. He has always set a good example and his priorities align with mine, which has been a good support in recent times. He had moved from the country to the city too, so he got it. Neither of us had the qualifications we needed but we had something just as powerful: we were both grafters. Jake taught me a lot, whether he knew it or not. Be humble. Be part of a team. Project good energy.

Now I had tackled work, I needed to find somewhere to live. I had no idea how difficult, hilarious and unnerving this would be. I scanned the adverts in the *Metro* newspaper and put the word around to colleagues and friends. The monthly rent for a room in a shared house was eye-watering, particularly to a girl from rural Cumbria. I went to look at a lot of tiny single bed-rooms in the houses of complete strangers and I would know as soon as I walked through the door that I couldn't live there. It was like being in a comedy, with faint hope being dashed in an instant. One guy told me what the rent was but that the deal also included me going out for dinner with him once a month.

Another said I could move in with him but he was a bodyguard for an Arabian prince, so if there were guns there then I wasn't to be alarmed. Red flags all over that, mate!

Just when I had almost given up, I found a room in a lovely house owned by a flight attendant, Alison. She was brilliant and hardly ever there. Neither was I, as I was making regular trips to Glasgow to see a boy and work meant I was all over the place. The arrangement worked well for us both. The house was in Twickenham, south-west London, which made it easy to get to Sky and the BBC – once I had navigated public transport. To this day, I still press the button to open the tube doors (even though they are automatic) and I talk to people when I get on the train. Apparently, that's what tourists do.

I took the same approach to story leads for BBC's *Newsround* and *Sportsround* as I had on previous jobs and got stuck in, ruffling a few traditional feathers in the process. I wasn't one of the stalwarts, nor was I one of the newcomers. I had this weird, invaluable experience to lean on from local radio and TV which set me apart. Five minutes before we were due on air, they would lock me out of the edit suite because I was always suggesting last-minute adjustments to news pieces or asking them questions in the hope I could learn more. It was an exciting time in sport, with the European Football Championship looming and the 2008 Beijing Olympics less than a year away. I felt settled and happy. When I walked through the iconic entrance at Television

Centre every day and partied in the city every weekend, I knew how lucky I was.

I got on really well with the editor of *Newsround*, Sinéad Rocks, who is still a good friend. A unique woman and talent, she was the perfect boss who could be harsh but was always fair. She was sarcastic but also supportive. She liked a laugh but always got the job done. She would push my chair from the news desk over towards the presenter's table and make me sit on what we called 'presenter's island'. She saw a potential in me.

Things were changing in the industry: digital TV was rapidly becoming more popular, and iPlayer was launched in the summer of 2007. A lot of people were joining a thing called Facebook. I was in a city I didn't really understand, surrounded by people who had totally different life experiences to me, and my family were a long way away. London is weird because you may only live a few miles from your mates but sometimes crossing the city after work feels like it takes the same effort as going abroad. I wasn't even comfortable in my own clothes. I was working in kids' television so I was no longer dressed like a middle-aged professional about to interview an MP. I had to find a wardrobe that worked for the role of 'big sister on screen' and use language that made conflict in Afghanistan appropriate for six-year-olds. I still smile when I think of encounters I had with BBC *News at Six* reporters at the scenes of incidents and disasters. There I was, from *Newsround,* having to convince a serious national news broadcaster that I should send my pictures before him. I was in baggy jeans and a Busted t-shirt, with a fringe I had cut myself, trying to put my case to the country's brightest brains. I always approached any disagreements with a 'kill it with kindness' mindset.

Sinéad was the one who pushed me to audition for *Blue Peter* and I said no. Don't get me wrong, I had huge respect for the programme, but I didn't think it was my thing. By this point, I thought I wanted to be Kate Adie. I wanted to go to war zones and file reports as bombs exploded behind me. I didn't want to sing and dance (which is ironic, considering my recent career highlights) and the Blue Peter presenters always seemed to be dressing up. Sinéad pulled me aside and told me, in no uncertain terms, that being a *Blue Peter* presenter was the best job on telly and if I didn't audition for it, she would sack me. I am still not sure if she was joking.

I will never forget the audition. I was faced with an assault course which was instantly appealing to a competitive, sporty girl like me. I hurtled through it as fast as I could, in and out of water, up and down obstacles, commando crawling under nets. All the while, the film crew kept trying to get me to talk on camera. They would ask me how it was going and how I felt, and I told them to shush because I was trying to get a good time! I didn't realise the point of the audition was for me to talk my way through the assault course and bring the viewer with me. I was just hell bent on being as speedy as possible, thinking the aim was to be fast, not entertaining. When I finished though, I thought, *Oh, this is the job, I get it now.*

There were also audition sessions in the studio. At one point, I had to make something and explain the process, which felt more like *Blue Peter* as I had imagined it to be. Then I was asked to sit with one of the cats on my lap. The phenomenal floor manager, Carmella Milne, brought over the big ragdoll cat, Socks, and, as she was about to hand it to me, I said, 'Oh I can't, I'm allergic to cats. I don't like them.' For a split second she looked shocked, and then she realised I was joking and burst out laughing. We really clicked. I think some of the other hopefuls had gushed about how much they loved cats and wanted to volunteer in a cat refuge or something. I have never been very good at playing that sort of game. To me, asking someone if they like animals was an odd question because surely everyone did? It was only with hindsight that I realise farm kids like animals in a different way to many people. We love them. We respect them. We live and work alongside them. But do we have t-shirts with pictures of cats on? No.

Joel Defries was another one of the auditionees and we really hit it off. He is one of the most ridiculously wonderful humans I have ever met. We couldn't be more different but we formed an instant sibling-style bond. I think this helped us both navigate the long audition process. There were various sessions where the auditionees would all be together, chatting about life ambitions and why we wanted the job. A lot of the talk was about world peace and charity work, and I wanted to interject and say, hang on, let's be realistic here, we want the job because we want to earn enough money to buy food and pay the rent, and because someone said this job came with a LOT of travel. I was torn about it, though. The assault course experience made me really want it but the studio sessions didn't feel like the right place for me to be. After a particularly dispiriting session, Joel and I escaped straight to the pub. I think this is what clinched the gig for us both because the producers saw us together and liked the fact that we got on.

A few days later, I was out running with a school friend (who years later created the international luxury brand Varley, which is an aside, but I always like to acknowledge my mate's successes) when one of the *Blue Peter* producers called me.

'Hi Helen, can I just ask you if you have any skeletons in your closet?'

'Nope.'

'Anything you wouldn't want to come out in the press?'

'Nope.'

'Any secrets you wouldn't want to share?'

'Nope.'

'OK, you've got the job.'

As you probably already knew, I really didn't have anything to hide.

I joined at the same time as the new editor, Tim Levell, who wanted to do the sort of stuff that really excited me. He wanted the programme to travel the world working with charities, supporting appeals and raising awareness for a variety of causes. Considering what I had initially thought, I couldn't quite believe that my TV work could also make a difference, that I could be proud of what I was doing and pay the rent. I was edging closer to my ambition of being Kate Adie.

Recently, someone in the industry said they had been a bit nervous of working with me because of my *Blue Peter* background, like it was a negative thing. Apparently, they had been happily surprised that I wasn't what they had expected. Maybe they had a preconceived idea of children's TV presenters. But let me say for the record how relevant, informative, entertaining and groundbreaking *Blue Peter* was and still is. It was ahead of the curve at so many points in its long history. The Manchester poet Tony Walsh said it so much better than me in a poem he wrote to celebrate *Blue Peter*'s sixtieth anniversary. If you have a moment, listen to it online in its glorious eight-minute entirety and remember why this show is iconic.

4

The New Girl

'It was one of the golden times in my life.'

Only a few weeks after I got the *Blue Peter* job, I was on a plane to Alaska with my co-presenters Joel and Ayo Akinwolere. We were flying out to spend six weeks filming our summer trip while the programme was on a seasonal break. Our exploits would then be slotted into the autumn series each week and inspire our viewers to explore the big wide world when they were older. It was an unbelievable experience. I'm talking helicopters, boats, snowmobiles, sledges and dangerous wildlife. Ambition, budgets and energy were big. With that came a degree of expectation, especially as the show was celebrating its fiftieth anniversary, so we did it in style by kayaking with whales, dangling out of helicopters and camping next to bears. It was brave and bold and I absolutely loved it. Above all, I was doing this with friends who immediately felt like family. Joel and Ayo became like brothers to me as we shared this wonderful and weird experience of being put in intense and challenging situations, while exploring our fears and thrills on camera.

Our onscreen chemistry matched our offscreen friendship and our personalities and attitudes complemented each other. I'll give you an example. We were standing on a glacier and the crew said, 'One of you is going to get lowered into this moulin (a vertical crack in the ice forming a crevasse) and will need to climb back out again. It is one of the most dangerous places in the world.'

'Fine,' I said, 'I'll do it.'

And the boys said, yes fine, she can do it. Nobody even attempted to talk me out of it or put themselves forward. From that moment, I became the adventurous one; Joel was funny and Ayo was creative, and the combination worked.

Early on, the three of us were given some presenter's training. The guy running it wanted to look at how we worked and interacted with each other. At the end of the session, he gave us feedback. I don't remember what he said about Joel but he told me I was so relaxed on television that I made other people nervous because they weren't sure what I was going to do next.

Then he turned to Ayo, and this bit I remember very clearly. He said, 'Ayo, I would love to know what your parents did because you are the most wonderful person.' And he was right. Ayo is charming in the truest sense of the word. The three of us could be on a plane and Ayo would be the one sitting next to a Swedish supermodel while Joel and I got the people who spilled their drinks everywhere, snored loudly and were a bit smelly. That boy could fall in a lake and come out with fish in his pockets.

A couple of years later, we did another summer expedition, this time to Turkey, which was one of the best trips of my life. We visited an archaeological dig in the middle of the desert. The archaeological students had been there for months so when we arrived with a crew they were beyond excited. It was enough for them to see new faces, let alone cameras. The director decided that part of the film segment needed Ayo and Joel to be dressed up like cave people in loincloths. Don't ask — it was very *Blue Peter* to be in costume. Anyway, Ayo looked incredible walking around like a Greek god, all glorious youth and muscle as the students chased after him. He was followed by Joel, who — and I hope he doesn't mind me saying this — was pale and lean, in something that looked more like a nappy. This was not his comfort zone. What was hilarious was being miked up and listening in to Ayo chatting to a girl, giving his best lines and singing song snippets. Joel, the sound man and I were in hysterics.

Ayo would confidently meet new people and make plans, but he wasn't the only one to enjoy flattering attention. I too met lots of interesting people, which would leave Joel moaning about how much more exciting our lives were than his. For instance, when we were filming in Italy, I went out for dinner with a truffle-hunting farmer in his Morgan sports car. Joel wanted to know why I got all the fun while he had dinner with the crew?! Not that they weren't fun but it was a different sort, if you know what I mean. When I think about the crew and the laughs we had, I stand taller. Take a bow Nigel Bradley, Darren Tate, Ryan Windley and Paul Stas – work friends who have popped up on various jobs throughout my career.

As our friendship played out on screen, so our roles were defined when the three of us competed in anything. Ayo would look really cool; I would win and Joel would be the comedy element. When we went to India, we took on a *Top Gear*-style challenge in Mumbai called 'Pimp My Tuk-Tuk'. We each had to decorate and style a tuk-tuk before riding it around the city touting for business. It was quite ridiculous, three kids' TV presenters trying to navigate the chaotic traffic and crowds of confused onlookers in our souped-up vehicles. Ayo transformed his with loads of colour, strong graffiti and a beatbox, which made it look super cool, and mine had a calming, yogic vibe with beautiful calligraphy. Joel had a bicycle. He didn't have a driver's licence so he wasn't allowed a motorised tuk-tuk. As Ayo and I were driving around, Joel was cycling up and down the hills of Mumbai with a paper picture of the Taj Mahal stuck on his bike. He was not happy, comfortable or speedy. Ayo and I were in hysterics.

We came back from one trip on which we had been away for a month working non-stop and yet it hadn't felt like work for a single second. Joel and I got off the plane and onto a tube at Heathrow and we sat on the train all the way to the end of the line and back again because we didn't want it to be over. We were both single, living in rented rooms in London and we had nothing to go home to.

Our job was to explore the world and film things that would excite, entertain and inform the audience back home. Sometimes, that's harder than it sounds when it comes to covering serious subject matters and events, like the 1986 nuclear power plant disaster in Chernobyl. Many years after the incident, I went to Ukraine with the *Blue Peter* team to film a piece about the football camp for the European Championships. While we were there, we wanted to weave in the story of the nuclear explosion tragedy in a way that would be appropriate for our young viewers. If anyone could get the balance right, *Blue Peter* could.

I remember, the nearer we got to the town, the stranger the

landscape became. At a huge perimeter fence, we had to go through airport-style security in makeshift military-looking buildings. It was eerily quiet. The closer we got to the site of the power plant, the more uncomfortable I felt. There is still a threat of radiation so we were only allowed as far as the landmark bridge where everyone had stood and watched the explosion. It was one of the oddest places I have been and the closest I have come to a scene of such awful devastation.

The surrounding town was unsettling too. It was as if time had stood still since the day the alarms went off and people left their homes thinking they would soon return. There were bikes abandoned on the street with weeds and grass smothering them. The Ferris wheel was mid-spin when it stopped. There were broken windows and doors standing open. Before we left, I saw a woman about the same age as my mum. It was strange to see her because there was nobody else on the streets and we had to get permission to be there. She was wandering aimlessly, muttering to herself, one of the few who had defied the advice not to return to their homes after the imminent danger had passed. It was a stark reminder that the unthinkable could happen.

Blue Peter had such a great reputation that doors would open, and by doors I mean Number Ten, Buckingham Palace and more. It was before YouTube was big so everyone from film stars like Jack Black to pop stars like Justin Bieber would come onto the show. Ed Sheeran even guest presented with me. It was one of the golden times in my life. Did I appreciate it as much as I should have? I hope so. If you're younger than me reading this, my advice is to enjoy whatever chapter you're in and don't waste it chasing what's next. There are amazing experiences in each part of our lives that we should value at the time, because circumstances inevitably change.

The show had such relevance and we rode that wave with a crew and production staff who were outstanding. Maybe it was particularly fun because Guitar Hero was always plugged in in the office and our editor played dance music from the speakers on his desk every Friday. Perhaps it was less stressful because the show was on a rolling commission with the BBC so we didn't have to worry about viewing figures or advertising revenues. The bottom line was it was a good time with good people. It's a cliché to say this but it was like being part of one big happy family. It was also an incredibly demanding 365-day contract which meant I had to expect and be willing to work any days but I was happy to do so. I didn't want a day off because I didn't want to miss out. Of course, we did get breaks but it was a unique working environment. I didn't have kids so my time was my own and I could be on location until late or stay an extra day if we met interesting people. It was all about making good telly and I swell with pride when people come up to me now and talk about the films I made for *Blue Peter*.

We would go from dogsledding in Inverness straight to Cornwall to learn how to surf with no chance to stop, catch our breath, eat or change our clothes. Occasionally, the production team had to go to my flat to pack a bag for me as I had no time to go home, and they would always put a face mask and a magazine on top. We would get back at midnight and sleep in the office because we were back out again at 6am the next day. We never knew when we were going home. Did we care? No, because it was what we wanted to do and if we didn't do it there would be someone else just as grateful for the opportunity to meet the Queen. Yes, the actual Queen.

It was the Commonwealth Games and *Blue Peter* was running a competition in conjunction with Buckingham Palace. We asked our audience to design a commemorative fifty-pence coin and there was a reception at the palace for the ten finalists. We went with them to film and have tea with Her Majesty. Ayo, Joel and I waited nervously in line to be presented to the Queen, trying to remember how we had been told to address her. She came to speak to Ayo first and then to me, but as I tried to respond she moved on to Joel, who said, 'Nice place you've got here.' She laughed! Amazingly, *Blue Peter* still had a great relationship with the palace after that, and with the House of Commons too. I could go in and have coffee with Black Rod (a senior official in the House of

Lords); I cleaned the Queen's throne for a filming segment and my mum got invited to the state opening of Parliament. It was a real testament to how trusted and respected the programme is, which is amazing when you think it is kids' telly. I don't mean that in a derogatory way; it just demonstrates the power and importance the show carries. I will be forever grateful for those experiences. My first ever Facebook post was a picture of me dressed up and ready to go to Buckingham Palace.

I think every past *Blue Peter* presenter believes their tenure was the best time, but I do feel we hit a sweet spot before social media became such a big thing. To mark the fiftieth anniversary, the time slot moved to 6pm on BBC One and the viewing figures were impressive. There was a lot of activity and press around this and I took part in my first ever photoshoot. It was for a Sunday supplement and involved all the past female *Blue Peter* presenters. What a baptism of fire, to do my first press piece surrounded by these women. Each amazing, each with character and presence. The first person I met when I turned up at the studio was Leila Williams (who presented the show from 1958 until 1962), who had a grace and dignity I can only aspire to. Some women just ooze class and she was one of them. It's hard to describe the atmosphere in that room. I think you have to be a certain type of personality to be a *Blue Peter* presenter – I say this with utter respect and also as one of them. Some of the women in there clearly loved the celebrations and their association while others felt obliged to be there. Some missed their badge-wearing, wing-walking days and others clearly couldn't wait to draw a line under it.

As a newcomer – to the show and photoshoots – I hung back. I may have imagined the feeling of hierarchy but I didn't rush to hair and make-up or the stylist's rail. I didn't really know what I was doing, either. I waited for everyone else to choose their dresses (and in a couple of instances, people took several outfits just in case) so by the time I got there, there was nothing smaller than a size 18. I had to wear a dress that was adjusted using bulldog clips. The stylist was so stressed and worried about my reaction; she was expecting a big drama to ensue. I really didn't care. It didn't make any difference to me. I was just happy to be surrounded by these women and be part of it all. It was my first experience of being with high-profile people and seeing how some could walk into a room and own it. It could have been a difficult environment with a clashing of egos, but instead there was a huge amount of warmth, love and camaraderie. Of course there was rivalry but it was amusing rather than intimidating, and helped by the pacifying presence of people like Lesley Judd and Janet Ellis.

Every one of us had our special moments and our connections with the show, and my fondness and delight at my link with this group continues to grow. My path often crosses with other *Blue Peter* alumni and many of us are in touch. It's not uncommon for Anthea Turner, Diane-Louise Jordan or Gethin Jones to message me if they sense I may not be having the shiniest day. Matt Baker never let me go to dinner alone when I was covering the Olympics and always invited me to join his group. I hugged Liz Barker when I saw her at *Strictly* as if she was my actual sister and it was only when I let go that I realised I had only met her a handful of times. When I kayaked down the Amazon, I received the most thoughtful note from Valerie Singleton congratulating me on my achievement and talking about me upholding the *Blue Peter* legacy. I treasured that message. *Blue Peter* is the strong bond that draws us together.

I remember hearing Britney Spears being interviewed and the interviewer was trying to provoke her into criticising Miley Cyrus. Britney played it brilliantly. She said something like, 'This is Miley's time. And as women we should support her, whatever mistakes she makes, and we should be excited for her because this is her time.' That message has stayed with me. It was relevant at the photoshoot all those years ago and it is still relevant now. I have been surrounded and supported by some of the most wonderful women – childhood mates, colleagues, new friends and family – and these relationships are some of the biggest blessings of my life. I hope my daughter finds the same as she grows up.

5

What Would Kate Adie Do?

'I came from a news background where it was about the unemotional facts, but I think one of my weaknesses in life has perhaps served me well. I am led by emotion.'

The first time I went to India was with *Blue Peter* and the charity Operation Smile. They are a non-profit medical service who perform operations on cleft lips and save many children's lives in the process. I couldn't wait to see first-hand the work they did, but I was totally unprepared for the country and the number of personal stories I discovered.

India wasn't at the top of my list of countries to visit but I fell head over heels in love with the place. It was like nowhere else I had ever been. Everything about it was so intense, from the weather, to the constant noise and the hustle and bustle of everyone around us. Travelling with a full camera crew meant we attracted attention everywhere we went. Before we started filming, I would have to hide in the car and wait for the crew to get in position. Then I would jump out and run to the other side of the road and back in the hope of confusing people to give me time to say my piece to camera.

Everyone working for Operation Smile was incredible. There were surgeons volunteering from all corners of the world. The American doctors were particularly open about their reasons for working with the charity, saying this was what they had trained for, not the incessant boob jobs for rich American housewives. In America, boob jobs paid big bucks, so they took the money, which afforded them time to do charitable work and eased their consciences. An admission that, if you thought about it too long, would make you ask a lot of questions, but the doctors I met seemed to be good people. Either way, their work in India was vital. Not only did this operation save lives by enabling children to eat properly, but some of these kids had never been out of their homes because due to the stigma surrounding cleft conditions. their families were ashamed of them. They thought they were cursed.

Consequently, there were queues and queues of parents with their children, desperate for them to be seen. They may have walked for eight hours, taken long bus journeys or slept on the floor of a hostel overnight, with no guarantee of an operation. The surgeons could only see a finite number of children and there were often four times as many patients as there were operation slots. How on earth do you choose between them?

On a couple of occasions, I was allowed to help administer the anaesthetic and was there when children came around after the operation to see their rebuilt faces for the first time. I was an emotional wreck and I didn't have kids at the time, so God knows what I would be like now. It made filming much harder for all the obvious reasons. We were sticking a camera into these people's lives but we were also trying to raise awareness at the same time. At one point, I was doing an emotional piece to camera and the sound man kept stopping me. He was picking up a squeak on the microphone and thought it might be my earring. After several attempts to work out what it was, I realised where the sound was coming from. I was being followed by a curious child in creaky shoes. I tried to explain what we were doing and promised I would play football with him as soon as I had spoken into the strange box!

Being in these places with a film crew is a mixed blessing. To make our charity appeal as impactful as possible, we wanted to focus on a few of the families who were waiting for operations. The parents were happy for us to film but I think they hoped this would enable their children to be bumped to the front of the queue. That wasn't how it worked and we followed their progress without any involvement, whatever the conclusion might be. The back stories took us on long drives to isolated communities where we stayed in places with no infrastructure, like running water or toilets. We had no idea what to expect, where we would be sleeping, what we would eat (or even if there was anything to eat), nor how we would be received. When we were in north-east India, the cameraman pulled up at the side of the road to get a wide shot of a field and within minutes thirty people had turned up from nowhere. I remember one little girl who had never been to school. She made chapatis with her dad and then took them out in a cart on the street to sell. That was her life.

I was so proud of the report we brought back from India and the way it galvanised our brilliant *Blue Peter* viewers. We encouraged them to make t-shirts which the hospital could use as hospital gowns for the children and then we took them back out to India with us. I still have a photo on my wall of the cameraman, sound man, producer and me, captured in a moment and forever in my memory.

Not every *Blue Peter* appeal had a fairy-tale script. In charity television appeals there are so many things to balance. Everything is open to interpretation and when the outcome affects people's lives, the stakes are high. Over the years, I have done a lot of appeal/charity filming with Comic and Sport Relief, often showcasing projects to illustrate where people's money went and who it benefited. One of the most memorable, for all the wrong reasons, was a trip to Bangladesh. We were working with Save the Children, among others, and trying to illustrate the extreme poverty in which children were living. Trying is the worst word ever. I will never forget the cameraman saying, 'Try not to look so shocked, this is their home.' I have never been good at hiding what I think or feel and I was floored.

I couldn't believe the extreme deprivation in the shanty towns and the conditions these children were living in. Families were stuck in cramped, rat-infested spaces with just a sheet to separate them from the next family, so a baby may be sleeping near someone dying of tuberculosis. We were filming with kids who were injured (I naïvely thought these injuries were accidental) and forced to beg on the streets. As a twenty-six-year-old who grew up in rural Cumbria, it was a big shock to the system. It is one thing knowing that this is reality for some and quite another witnessing it happening in front of you.

I became part of the Comic Relief family around the same time and went to Sierra Leone. We were filming with kids whose lives had been ripped apart by the civil war and were living on the streets. Their community had been devastated by the fighting and they had lost family and infrastructure. No sewerage pipes. No running water. There was a boy who had to walk miles to get water from a well and we filmed his progress; on the way back, he trod on glass and cut his foot badly. The crew said we needed a wide shot and a close shot, but by this point I had seen enough. I told the child to get on my back so I could carry him and I told the crew to stop filming and help. If they could carry a tripod, they could carry a bucket of water. The cameraman, Paul, who is still a good friend of mine, said, 'And that's why we love you, Helen, because you think you can change the world, but we are here filming because we can show it back at home and make everyone else want to change the world too.' He was right. It was a hard lesson to learn but it was an important one if I was going to continue working on charity appeals. That said, I didn't put the boy down. As we walked through one village, these guys shouted out, 'Hey, Madonna! Stop stealing our kids!' To this day, I don't quite know what to make of that.

On the same trip, we were filming children who were dying from diarrhoea and we wanted to convey the seriousness of what happens without fresh water. We were in a hospital and I was in the room when a child passed away, surrounded by his parents and doctors. I was there to do my job so I turned to the camera and spoke from the heart. At the end, the producer said, 'That was great, Helen, but can you do it again? You forgot to put the phone number on the end.' I just looked at him. I couldn't believe he had asked me. I had already felt

I shouldn't be there, let alone be filming, but I had the brave parents' consent and I knew it was important to show these devastating moments. If this didn't make people at home pick up the phone and pledge their hard-earned money, what would? The cameraman put the camera on the floor and said, 'We're done here.' Yes, we were there to make a programme about what was happening in order to raise money to help stop it, but it was still happening right in front of us and we needed to respect people's lives.

Looking back, I think I was probably too young for that assignment and to be able to understand the landscape of what I was doing. I was in a room with a child who had just died. We were filming and I was supposed to do a piece to camera. So, what was my responsibility? To report on this or to respect the situation? Paul was right, we were making something to bring back so everyone at home could really understand the truth of what was happening in Sierra Leone. This was our best chance of getting donations, which would ultimately benefit more children than just the one I had carried back to his village. Yet, when you are in that situation and you have a real person in front of you who is dying or needs help, what do you do? What would Kate Adie do?

Now that I am a mother, I often wonder what I would do now and how I would behave faced with the same dilemma. I came from a news background where it was about the unemotional facts, but I think one of my weaknesses in life has perhaps served me well. I am led by emotion. One of my strengths is to connect with people and tell their stories. There are times when things have gone wrong in my life and I don't mind that it plays out publicly because it may help some people to see that if I am OK then they will be too.

Recently, when I was presenting BBC's *Morning Live* with Gethin Jones, we were interviewing a father about his son's cancer diagnosis. Beforehand, it was agreed that as presenters we shouldn't get too emotional because that's not our job – our job is to share the story and focus on the facts. But I was visibly upset during the interview and I said something brief to the dad about every parent being on his team and right behind him. Once we were off air, whether or not I should have said that was discussed in the debrief. In fact, the producers agreed with my ad-lib, which is why I love being part of the show. It's a programme for real people made by people who are not afraid to show real emotions and I think the viewers at home respond to this.

I am a heart-on-my-sleeve sort of person and I can't be any other way. Comic Relief took me and the presenter Steve Jones to

Uganda, where we filmed with children who lived on the streets in unimaginable situations, dealing with things including substance abuse and sexual exploitation. They were sleeping on the side of the dual carriageway and alternating between begging and robbing people. One of the initiatives Comic Relief supported was a school for these kids and the success rate was high once they got them through the door. It was going well but there was still a lot of work to be done and I wanted to speed things up. I remember spouting off to Steve about what we should be covering in the report and he said 'no, this is not how this plays out, we cannot interfere here.' He was brilliant. He understood why we were there and how we could use our power in a way that I was still learning about.

While we were there on the streets, the cameraman suggested I go to the other side of the dual carriageway so he could film the traffic whizzing past in front of me, to illustrate how dangerous the road was. We all agreed it would make a great shot. I crossed three lanes of busy traffic to the other side as they got ready to film. I got mugged. Unsurprising, really. I'm not sure what we were thinking. The crew watched helplessly as someone grabbed me, yanked at my cheap necklace and legged it. The street erupted with fury. We were bundled into a car and driven off. The sound man was more traumatised than I was because he had been able to hear everything that was happening to me through my discreet microphone. He kept saying he'd wanted to get to me, but there had been three lanes of speeding traffic in the way. It was a stark reminder that we had stepped into a world that we couldn't control. Being in a film crew didn't keep us safe.

One of the things I admire about Comic Relief is how close we, as TV presenters and actors, get to the funded projects and how respectful the organisation is of the people involved. In the UK, I filmed with a twelve-year-old girl whose mum had schizophrenia. The girl attended a Comic Relief-funded youth club which was a lifeline for her. In the interview, she was very open about her mum's illness and how it impacted her – it was an incredibly powerful, raw piece. We watched the edit and thought, *How will she feel about this in a few years? Is she going to be happy she did this?* In the end, we didn't show it. She was only twelve. I think that was the right thing to do.

I am incredibly proud of the charity appeals and fundraising I have been part of over the years. I loved every one of the experiences and have the most amazing memories. I feel at home with this sort of immersive journalism. For all the interviews with famous people (and I am more than happy to do those too!) this is the work that inspires me. It is what I hoped to be involved with when I joined *Blue Peter* and I was thrilled to be part of so many appeal trips. I love sharing other people's stories. Working in telly, it can be hard not to disappear inside your own head or get seduced by great opportunities offering lots of money, but I continue to remind myself why I am doing this job.

6

As Easy as Riding
a . . . Skateboard

*'I always say there is a fine line between bravery
and stupidity; I have pushed that line at times.'*

When I agreed to take part in the UK Women's Downhill
Skateboarding Championships, I hadn't been on a skateboard
since I was a child. It was my first big physical challenge for
Blue Peter and I assumed, a bit like riding a bike, that it would
all come back to me. I couldn't have been more wrong. I was
terrified as soon as I picked up speed and continually fell off the
skateboard during the practice sessions. I was covered in painful
bruises to prove it. In the run-up to the event, I was convinced

I was going to seriously hurt myself. I thought of Mum in the yard at home all those years before, attempting to have a go on my skateboard. Now I knew how she'd felt.

I think the skateboard is one of those metaphors for life. You have to commit to riding one because as soon as you feel scared, you become tense, which makes you wobble, and the more you wobble, the more likely you are to fall off. It's like being trapped in a vicious circle of fear where everything seems impossible. I learned the hard way that the best approach is to take a deep breath, quieten the saboteur voices in my head and focus on what I had to do, then I would be more likely to achieve it. This is one of the techniques I have picked up over years of facing difficult situations and trying to find what works for me. However, I do appreciate that this is easier said than done – particularly if you are standing on a thin piece of wood attached to four small wheels.

I didn't get a single wink of sleep the night before the challenge. The words of the coach I had been working with ricocheted around my brain. Early on in my training, he had said something life-changing to me: 'If you can do this, you can do anything.'

And I thought, *This is what I want. I want to be physically strong, emotionally free and able to focus on tackling whatever life throws at me. If this is how I achieve it, by careering down a steep hill on a skateboard without throwing up or breaking several bones,*

then bring it on. Well, OK, I didn't really think 'bring it on'.
I was so full of anxiety and nerves I probably would have
pulled out if I hadn't been filming it for the programme.
Instead, I was very aware that I was one small cog in a *Blue
Peter* wheel and the team had persuaded the UK Women's
Downhill Skateboard Championships to let me, a total rookie,
take part. Not only that, I was also working with a coach who
had put his reputation on the line to teach me to skateboard.
None of this was lost on me. Neither was the young audience
who would watch my journey and know that if I could do
hard things then so could they.

The championships were held at Beachy Head in Sussex, so
when I say 'downhill', I mean down a hill. I was dressed in full
motorcycle leathers and a crash helmet – that's how dangerous
it was – and I was absolutely petrified. I wouldn't say I am
the sort of person who needs to be under pressure to perform,
but I did have a moment just before the race started when
I regained control in my head and told myself I was just going
to do it. And against the odds, I did. Somehow, I got from the
top to the bottom in a heart-in-mouth flash without falling off.
The relief and exhilaration was overwhelming and I ran over
to hug my coach at the end. *Now I can do anything!* I thought.
Hilariously, because of the way the championship rankings
work, I was fourth in the UK for a few days, but there was no
time to celebrate. Still in motorcycle leathers, I had to jump

straight into a car to Heathrow Airport, walk through security and catch a flight to the Isle of Wight where I was competing in the powerboat championships.

This was what my exciting life was like with *Blue Peter*. Nigel Bradley, the amazing cameraman, told me I had to make the most of every opportunity that was thrown at me in the job and he was absolutely right. What was to follow pushed me further than I'dever thought possible, but the skateboard challenge was a big turning point in my career and for me personally. I always say there is a fine line between bravery and stupidity; I have pushed that line at times, but somehow it has all worked out in the end. Leading up to the race, I realised it was OK to be scared sometimes, even too intimidated to sleep and too anxious to eat. They are awful, complex emotions but once you acknowledge them and continue to put one foot in front of the other, you will be OK. Sometimes you just have to keep going. It's as simple as that.

The day I pushed off on that skateboard at Beachy Head, I didn't know if I was going to make it through but I held the tiniest hope that I might. And that was enough. If there's a chance, however small, I think it is worth leaning into a decision that might turn out to be the bravest thing you ever do.

7

Marathon Woman

'I wanted to be battle-ready for life. And so I ran and I ran.
Until my toenails fell off and my ribs bled.'

The next big challenge I took on was my own silly fault. The *Blue Peter* production team was considering ideas and asked Joel, Ayo and me what would take each of us out of our comfort zones. Ayo was terrified of water, so he learned how to swim and faced his fear by front-crawling across the Mariana Trench, the deepest part of the Pacific Ocean. I was so damn proud of him. Joel was desperate for an exotic trip, so he suggested learning to scuba-dive in the Maldives. He was thrilled when they agreed, except his cunning plan backfired because he had to do all his training in dark, freezing water in Southampton.

As for me, I said I had always wanted to do the Marathon des Sables, running 250km over six days in the Moroccan Sahara. Never having run a marathon, I was in awe of the people who took part in this event, but it wouldn't work with the programme's schedule because it would mean taking more than a week off presenting the show. Instead, the production team found the closest thing that would work, which was a Namibian ultra-marathon where you ran three marathons. In the desert. Within twenty-four hours.

Now, let me be very clear at this point. I was not a runner by any stretch of the imagination. I had done a half marathon once in a stupidly slow time and that was the extent of my experience. I started *Blue Peter* in the summer of 2008, began training for the marathon in December and was due on a flight to Namibia three months later, so time was of the essence. I went back to my parents' farm for Christmas and attempted my first training run. I limped around one of their fields for ten minutes and could hardly breathe. Daunted and deflated, I walked back into my parents' kitchen, where they took one look at my sad face and said, 'Do you think this is a good idea?'

At this stage, I thought it was a terrible idea too but I had committed to the challenge and I was determined. From that moment on, I ran whenever and wherever I could. What began as a half run/half walk got a bit quicker as I kept going. I would jog, walk, shuffle – anything to get the miles in my legs. If I finished work late I would go straight to the gym and run on the treadmill until they kicked me out at closing time. Instead of getting public transport I would run everywhere. I lived near the River Thames so I would run to Hammersmith, where a friend or work colleague would join me for a while as I ran all the way to Brixton. Or I would get to Clapham, turn around and run in the opposite direction to Richmond.

In truth, I didn't have anything else to do outside of work as most of my friends were still back in Cumbria. I didn't work regular hours so I didn't have a social circle, and I was distracting myself from a humiliating situation involving my Scottish footballer ex-boyfriend who, according to a national newspaper, had been sexting a glamour model. She then sold her story to the *News of the World,* so I was on the front of the Scottish newspapers for a couple of weeks. It wasn't my first time waking up to see my face and personal photos in a newspaper, but it was the first time the content could also humiliate my parents and brother. That hurt and it's not something I have ever been comfortable with. I can't complain about any part of my job but I don't like anything that reflects badly on my family or causes them embarrassment. They are private, gracious people who will stand by me no matter what, but it's only now I have kids that I can see how deeply affected they are by anything written about me. It's probably my brother who I owe the biggest apology to as he still moved in the same circles as my ex. I am just pleased to say all footballers ended that chapter of our lives with their legs intact.

So, the marathon challenge came at exactly the right time. I was upset about the end of the relationship and the way it had happened, and I thought, *If I train really hard, it will train me for life.* I wanted to do something physically painful so I had a reference point for the next time I was thrown something really shit to deal with. I wanted to face myself and see how far I could be pushed. I figured this marathon could be my marker for the future, my way of saying, *Think that's bad? I have got through something way harder.* I wanted to be battle-ready for life. And so I ran and I ran. Until my toenails fell off and my ribs bled from the chaffing of my sports bra, but I didn't care because I was slowly turning into a runner.

I trained with a great coach, Rory Coleman, who had run many ultra-marathons and was a brilliant mentor. He took me to my first marathon, which was running the Circle Line tube above ground in London, and *Blue Peter* filmed it. It was a real team effort with various members of production running with me at different points and cheering me on from landmarks. I was incredibly slow and the poor camera crew would get short shrift if they asked me to go back because they had missed a shot, as it was the last thing I wanted to do.

Most of that challenge was filmed by a wonderful man called

Eric McFarland, a TV talent and top bloke, who has seen me through several challenges and at some of my very, very lowest points on and off camera. There were also occasions when the team would spring surprises on me, on camera, to capture my very real reaction. One particular horror was when I ran a half-marathon, got to the finishing line and Rory said, 'Well done! Now, guess what? Turn around because we're doing it in reverse.' I was miked up and told the crew exactly what I thought of them as I retraced my steps over another thirteen miles. It became so commonplace for the production team to spring surprises on the presenters that we were always in a state of mild anxiety, braced for what they were going to do next!

To prepare for the heat of Namibia I did a training run in Morocco, which was also filmed for *Blue Peter*. We picked a pretty remote rural area so the camera crew marked the roads with chalk paint so I could see the route I needed to follow. Then they would drive a few miles ahead, ready to film me as I approached, sweaty and tired. Unfortunately, the local people thought the marks meant that a tarmac road was coming, so they were furious and shouted at me as I ran past. I tried to explain, unsuccessfully, why I was there. It was easier when I was back in Cumbria, where I attempted my longest run of fifty miles and finished to cheers from family and friends after twelve hours. After three months of training, I had covered a total distance of 747 miles, trained for 190 hours and run ten marathons in that time. I was as ready as I was ever going to be.

Five thousand miles away from home, I was excited and in awe of Namibia; it was stunningly beautiful. There was a minor hiccup when we got there and discovered we didn't have the correct visas so we were detained. The officials said they would sort something out the following day, but by then it would have been too late and I would have missed the beginning of the race. Though it felt bonkers to be begging them to hurry the process because I wanted to run seventy-eight miles through a desert! They solved the problem and we were released in the nick of time.

I arrived at the camp where we were staying the night before and met the other twenty-three runners taking part in the race. They were as lean and fit as racehorses, wearing skinny leggings and wraparound sunglasses, looking like proper runners. I was in a polka-dot boob-tube dress and wedge sandals, and I had a mass of plaited hair extensions. I kid you not. I immediately felt like a fish out of water. I said hello to people in an embarrassed, shoulder-shrugging, 'Hi, I'm running too! Gonna give it a whirl!' manner. They must have thought I had no chance. I would have agreed with them at that point.

We double-checked the kit we were carrying in our bags. There seemed an awful lot of it: food, cooking equipment, first-aid kit, second pair of trainers. I also had to carry a tracker device about the size of a bag of sugar so the *Blue Peter* audience back home could follow my progress. Most importantly, I had to make sure I had enough water to get me to the first checkpoint. These stations were at thirteen-mile intervals. When we reached them we would be weighed to make sure we weren't seriously dehydrated and could then refill our water bottles. Before we went to bed in our tents, there was a medical debrief which left me in no doubt of the extreme nature of this endurance test: the medic listed dehydration, muscle cramps, vomiting and sunstroke as possible complications. The enormity of the challenge suddenly hit me. We were all camping next to the start line ready for the race to begin, a nervous bunch which consisted of a couple of women but mainly men older than me. I chatted to three runners who had run it previously, including a brilliant Irish guy who had won it the year before. I asked him about the heat. His answer will stay with me forever. He said, 'Helen, it's so hot, it's like running through a wall of fire.'

Camping in the Namibian desert is an experience in itself, without waking up and attempting to run nearly eighty miles. The first few miles were over long grass and we had been warned about snakes who would be woken by the sound of feet trundling along a normally quiet stretch of sand. After months of preparation I was pleased to be on my way, but by 9am it was already brutally hot. Of course, the excitement meant most people went thundering off, some capable of that kind of pace, others not. I was not and immediately found myself near the back of the pack, keeping an eye out for snakes.

Within an hour, the heat claimed its first casualty with one of the runners dropping out, followed by several more before we had reached our first checkpoint. By the middle of the day, it was 43 degrees in the desert. The landscape was vast and intimidating, the heat so intense any exposed skin felt like it was on fire, even with factor fifty on. My legs were the colour of boiled lobsters and I was so dehydrated, I was hallucinating wind turbines looming over me and seals crossing the road. Before we had completed one marathon, participants were being pulled from the race and I was still at the very back of the pack. This was not good because the organisers would pick up the stragglers, knowing they wouldn't be able to finish within the twenty-four-hour timeframe. I did not want to risk being pulled off the race, so this was stressful in itself.

The *Blue Peter* crew were amazing. The cameramen Nigel and Darren and the producers Eric and Kieran would run bits of the race with me, film and then jump back into the truck and drive on ahead. It became intense really quickly. At one point, desperate for shade and a brief break, I crouched down behind a bush. Mentally, I was in a really dark place and I thought I was going to lose it. The crew swarmed, camera in my face, keen to catch me battling my demons because it makes really good telly. They wanted me to tell them how I felt. Instead, I said, 'Can you fuckers just look me in the eye and tell me I can do this?! Tell me I am going to be fine!'

It was the weirdest feeling. I wanted them to be my friends first and my work colleagues second. They wanted to look after me but they had to capture my breakdown because it was their job. As I rejoined the race, the crew ran back to their van and I spotted a fridge through the window. They had a FRIDGE and it was full of cans of ice-cold Coca-Cola! It was the one thing I craved but couldn't have until after the race because you were only allowed to consume what you were carrying. It felt like the ultimate betrayal and as I ran past them, I screamed, 'I hope you fucking choke on that!' I'm pleased to say that all four men are still really good friends of mine.

It took me nine hours to run the first marathon. By this point, six runners had dropped out. My feet were a mess – they were covered in blisters the size of fifty-pence pieces and all my toenails had fallen off. I felt like I was running on razor blades. The blisters were so raw and open that every step was agony. I shuffled for several miles on tiptoe, yelping with pain every time my feet hit the sandy, rocky desert floor. Years later, I was reminded of the feeling when I was breastfeeding for the first time and it felt like someone putting hot nails through my toes.

The worst thing about doing this stuff on telly is you can't get out of it – though it's also the best thing. To boost morale,

Eric gave me a pile of letters from viewers saying how much they believed in me and knew that I was going to finish the race. That was the impetus I needed to get me back on my feet for the second marathon. I couldn't let them down. This time, it wasn't the heat that was the problem. Because it was night, it was pitch black. I had a head torch to help but I had ten hours of darkness ahead of me. I was also one of the last runners so I knew if I didn't pick up the pace I would be pulled out of the race.

At 10pm, I arrived at the halfway checkpoint, thirty-nine miles in. Looking around at the other runners, I could see the toll the race was taking. I loved running with different people and hearing their reasons for pushing themselves in such an extreme way. Some were seasoned runners; others were doing it for their mental health. One guy I ran alongside for a while had been in Hurricane Katrina and suffered from panic attacks. He had taken on the challenge to prove to himself he could do it. He told me he had fallen apart emotionally and physically in front of his wife and needed something to prove to himself he was strong again.

A third of the field had dropped out by now. As each person gave up, I knew exactly what the crew were thinking, and probably every other runner too. Nobody thought I was going to finish. They had written me off. A couple of runners even told me I wouldn't do it so to make sure I just enjoyed the experience for as long as I was in it. That was the kick up the backside I needed. I took a couple of paracetamols and got back out there. As numbers dwindled at each checkpoint stop, it highlighted just how tough the challenge was, but it also motivated me to keep going.

Around the forty-mile mark, my blisters reduced me tears and through gritted teeth, I repeated the mantra, 'I am not going to quit.' Amy, one of the medics, turned up in her van and had a good look at my feet, popping my blisters and retaping my toes. It didn't make any difference and, for the first time, I considered stopping. I turned to the camera and said I just couldn't do it. I didn't think I could go on. It was 2am and I had covered forty-seven miles. Every part of my body ached, I felt sick and I was exhausted. My running shoes were stained with blood. But still, the thought of giving up was worse. The look on the camera crew's faces hurt more than my blisters or burning muscles. They shared a look of pity tinged with disappointment. It's one I have seen many times since then and it's not a feeling I have ever been comfortable with. To see people who love you feeling disappointed for you is soul-destroying. When people back you and support you, you don't want to let them down. It's not something I will ever get used to and it is a feeling that will always make me dig deeper and appreciate the people in my life. Without good people beside us, what do we do these things for anyway?

I knew the fourth checkpoint was an hour away and if I could get there, I would be two thirds of the way through the race. I wasn't thinking about the end; I just didn't know how to stop. I kept thinking about how it would feel to say I didn't finish and until I could work out what to tell the expectant team back at *Blue Peter,* who had run all those miles with me for all those months, I couldn't stop.

There were no other runners when I arrived at checkpoint four. I was half an hour behind everyone else and it was touch and go as to whether I would be allowed to continue. I was now in a race against time as well as my own stamina and if I didn't speed up, I would be out. It would mean I would have gone through all the agony for nothing. I had been running for eighteen hours, I still had a marathon left to do and I would need to run it faster than any marathon I had ever done. When I put it like that it sounds mad I know, but there was a fighting spirit in me that needed to see how far I could go.

I shuffled on. At one point, a support vehicle went past me and I could see the guy who had been affected by Hurricane Katrina sitting in the back. He had either pulled out or been stopped. I didn't know which, but it made me cry.

At 5.30am, I was sixty-one miles in and coming up to checkpoint five. At earlier stop-offs I had taken an hour to eat and rest, but there was no chance for this now so I allowed myself only a few minutes before setting off again. The final stretch was the worst because I had been running on sand and gravel up to this point and now I was limping on a tarmac road. My feet were absolutely done in. The film crew perked up. They could suddenly see the possibility of me completing the race and were like, 'Sod the TV programme, she just needs to finish this!' The sound man went above and beyond by popping my blisters and taping up my feet. And Nigel gave me a rallying pep talk about only having thirteen miles left and running at such-and-such a pace. They believed in me. I believed in me.

After a while, though, I thought, *Surely I should be nearly finished by now?* From the van, Nigel shouted out, 'Oops, sorry! I got that wrong, it was sixteen miles so just a few more to go.' And they sped off with me shouting, 'You bastards!' at them.

With just ten minutes to spare, I crossed the finish line after twenty-three hours and fifty minutes. I don't think I have ever been so physically and emotionally broken, either before or since. I came eighth out of the twenty-three people with whom I had started the race. I don't know how many people finished, but I remember seeing the winner on a drip in the shade of a car. *Blue Peter* had flown out my mum to greet me at the finish line, which was the most wonderful surprise, particularly because she doesn't like long-haul flights. I found out the logistics people had had a bet on as to when I would drop out. Not if, but when.

When I had started running, a few months previously, I was

unable to last more than ten minutes, but I kept going because I wanted to prove something to other people. I naïvely thought I could run eighty miles, no problem. But there were plenty of problems and it very quickly became about proving something to myself. I needed to know I had more in the tank when I felt I didn't. I needed to push through the dark times and learn it's possible to come out of the other side. And thank God I learned this lesson.

After the race, I was fine for twelve hours and then I crashed. My hair was so matted it had to be cut off when I got back to London. My feet were ruined and I carried my toenails around in my purse for months. This is weird, I know, but I wanted to remind myself of what I had achieved. I don't think people talked about mental health then like they do now. I know that race took me to places in my head that I had never been before. People asked me if it was harder or easier to take on the challenge for TV and I think it was harder because I carried the weight of everyone's hope and expectation. That said, I may have stopped if I hadn't been under that immense pressure. My final piece to camera was a message to all the children watching. Euphoric and exhausted, I said, 'You know what, if anyone says you can't do anything, just get your head down and get on with it because you probably can.'

*   *   *

Two weeks later, I ran the London Marathon so I could report from it for Radio 5 Live. I knew I had the best excuse in the world to get out of it, but as I reasoned to myself, when would I ever run a marathon again and say, oh, ONLY twenty-six miles?! It felt amazing to jog in cool April weather and be surrounded by crowds of people who cheered as I went past. The ultra-marathon had been incredibly lonely at points. I always say mass participation makes you like people. On the start line of the London Marathon, or any big event like the Great North Run, there's such a weird camaraderie as you all will each other to do well. It's emotional, nerve-wracking and very humbling to see people running for family and friends they have lost and illnesses they have conquered.

A couple of years later, I ran the London Marathon again for BBC Sport and was filmed throughout, doing the coverage at the start of the day, chatting with other runners and crossing the finish line. I was a bit quick at the end because I was desperate to come in before the programme came off air. I sprinted over to the cameraman and said my piece live to camera, which was probably a bit garbled, and then promptly threw up all over him. Apparently everyone in the gallery stood up and cheered!

The last time I ran the London Marathon, I did a proper training schedule with the legendary runner Steve Cram. In the debrief afterwards, he printed off my splits and questioned my progress, asking why I had slowed down at mile eighteen.

I said, 'I was having a good time, Steve, I am not an athlete! I was probably having a couple of jelly babies.'

One year, I ran the New York Marathon and my friends said they would come to support me, but they were having the time of their lives so they missed me at various points, although they met me at the end. I will never forget one of them, Karen, saying as soon as she saw me, 'Oh my God, my feet are killing me, we've been walking around New York all day!' I said, 'Karen, I have just run a marathon.' And her response? 'Well, you've got trainers on. I'm in boots.' They wanted to go straight to Saks Fifth Avenue and I said my feet were hurting. 'Oh come on, Helen,' they chorused, 'we're in New York!'

In the Lake District, I did two marathons on consecutive days, for which I ran along Scafell Pike, the highest peak in England. I am tempted to do 'the Bob Graham', which is forty-two peaks in twenty-four hours. Though I haven't looked into this further because I don't have time to take on the training with three small children to look after. But I know there are a few women with kids who have done it so that has inspired me to consider it in the future. I am also friends with Steve Cram and Ali Curbishley, who keep nudging me to return to marathon life. Maybe I will. I run to keep my head, not my arse, peachy. Besides, after every London Marathon I message friends and say, 'Shall we do it next year?!'

8

Kayaking the Amazon (By Accident)

'I don't think I truly appreciated the strength I got from being in nature back then. Now I realise that when I am in those environments it feels like coming home.'

Sport Relief came knocking. They had got wind of my Namibian adventures and asked if I fancied doing a challenge for them. They were keen to film one of their projects in South America and tie in an adventure at the same time. They had come to the right girl. It was an absolute privilege to be asked and my mind whirred with thoughts of what could be ahead for me. There were various discussions between Sport Relief and *Blue Peter* before it was suggested I do something in the Amazon.

Maybe I could kayak down a section of the Amazon River? 'Why part of it?' I said, 'I may as well do it all. That will have more impact.' At this point, I had no idea how long or dangerous the Amazon was, but I did have work mates who were as enthusiastically naïve as I was. Matt, Gav and Anne Marie were just three of a work army who would egg me on and tell me it wasn't mad or stupid to do something so mad or stupid.

This set off a series of meetings involving Colin Pereira, who was head of the BBC's High Risk Team at the time, and thought it was a terrible idea, so I should have known then what I was letting myself in for. I went to the health and safety meeting and everyone was asking each other whether it was possible. Should we do this? Could we make it happen? Colin said he wasn't sure it could be done. I was like the girl at school who got in trouble with the headmaster for asking too many questions and being facetious. I said, 'Yes Colin, but should I try?!'

We went around the room with everyone saying what they thought. I think she can do this! No, she can't! Well, I think she can! It finally got to me and, with a glint of adventure in my eyes, I said, 'OK, whether I can or can't is irrelevant because I am not on the Amazon yet, nor have I ever been in a kayak. But should we try?' And again Colin said no.

It felt like all was lost at this point. Tim Levell, my editor at *Blue Peter,* was a brilliant boss and a fantastic editor, and I hope he won't mind me saying that he was also endearingly bonkers at times. He went to senior management meetings on occasion in fancy dress and he would always say what was on his mind. Like many creatives, he was great to work with and frustrating to work for. Good television is made by some of these people. He would usually encourage my daredevil attitude and make things happen, but at this point he said, 'Helen, there is no way you can take this on.' Day after day I would sit by his desk trying to persuade him to reconsider, but everyone else was telling him it was impossible. Yet, the more people told him it was impossible, the more he started to think, *Yes, but what if she pulls this off?!* Rowing the length of the Amazon River? It could be epic. He worked out the budget and said, 'OK, let's try and make this happen.' If it hadn't been for the unfailing belief Tim had in me, coupled with his ability to turn over many a BBC stone to find the budget we needed, I would never have experienced one of the best, most life-enhancing and exhausting adventures of my life.

It was then that I discovered I would need to paddle around 2,010 miles. Not only did the Amazon run through three countries, it also crossed an entire continent. Plus, it was tidal, and five miles wide at some points. Someone dismissed the challenge as me just being a giant Pooh stick washed down the river without making any effort, but this wasn't the case. The tide would mean I would have to work for my progress. I had never been in a canoe or kayak and I didn't know how hard it was.

Kayaking the Amazon (By Accident)

The first time I got in a kayak I fell straight out. Luckily, I was being coached by a GB kayak instructor, Mark Hoile, who was brilliantly supportive and creative in his approach to preparing me for the extreme environments I would be facing. He arranged for me to have an ergo rowing machine so I could practise in my living room, as well as doing weights in the gym. I was flat-sharing in London with one of my best mates from home, Rebecca, who was always supportive but often bemused by my strange life. She would say, 'I have no idea why they create all these challenges for you to film when your real life is just as chaotic. Even the simplest of things turn into an adventure without you even trying.' And yet she always put up with walking into our flat to see me me, when I came back from Mumbai or wherever I had been, sitting on a rowing machine with the kettle boiling on repeat with the lid off, so that it replicated a steamy, hot and humid environment. She is one of those friends who will always be like family, no matter how little I see her.

With Rebecca's help – and she is half the size of me – we hauled the cumbersome ergo into a hire van so I could drive the thing home for Christmas and continue to train on my days off. While we were trying to manoeuvre it, I got mugged and lost my handbag full of Christmas gifts and priceless photos from a trip to India. Thus proving that chaos always seems to find me.

Over the festive period, friends would come round to see me and, while I rowed, they sat drinking gin and tonic. I was so conscious of the task at hand that I wanted to train whenever I could but I didn't have enough time off to focus on it. On a filming trip to India, I took a medicine ball with me so I could continue to exercise. It caused a right old upset at Indian customs because they didn't know what it was and I wasn't sure how to explain it. Training was tough and the doubts began to build, but I had relentlessly pursued this opportunity and now that everyone was making it happen, I couldn't pull out.

We flew to Peru at the beginning of January 2010 and, yet again, the film crew who came with me were outstanding, including Gav, Stu, Ben, Lucy the doctor and Eric, the director who had been with me in Namibia. Eric believed in me more than I deserved. He always has. Like a member of my family, his loyalty and support were unquestioning.

Before we began the challenge, we went to a Sport Relief project which helped children who spent their days on rubbish tips, scavenging for scrap to sell. It was important to show people where their donations were going and the visit was exactly the motivation I needed as we prepared for the challenge ahead. Then we took a plane to an airfield, where we got on a smaller plane to Iquitos and took a river boat to the point I was to start from. As the true source of the Amazon River is a stream up in the mountains, we chose an alternative beginning – the place where the Marañón and Ucayali rivers converge. I had my tiny kayak and the crew had a big boat for us all to sleep on.

Kayaking the Amazon (By Accident)

For forty-two days, I spent sixteen hours a day, sunrise to sunset, on the water. I was adamant that all I wanted to do was sit in my kayak, cross off the miles and get it done. As usual, I was so fixated on the challenge that I would often forget I was also doing it for the telly. Some days, we would have to stop to go and film in the jungle because we needed the content to break up the relentlessness of watching me paddling for hours on end. I found this frustrating but I knew it would make the programme even better. I had taken an iPod which broke early on, meaning I was listening to JLS and Cheryl Cole on repeat. One day, Eric told me he had a present for me. He had bought a headdress from a village we had stopped off at and he wanted to film me wearing it. I said, 'Eric, is this a present or is this for filming? Because they are two different things.' And he said, 'Well, it's a present but I want to film it.' So I replied, 'That means it's not a present then, doesn't it? It makes it a prop.' I loved working with Eric.

Every Saturday, I was live on BBC *Breakfast*, giving updates from my kayak. All credit to the team for making the technology work because we were in the middle of the rainforest and we didn't even know exactly where we were some of the time. Parts of the Amazon aren't mapped. Yet we could still broadcast live television. It's mad to think of it now but FaceTime wasn't a thing then, so we were really testing the tech as well as ourselves. And our regular catch-ups were not only interesting for the viewers but also for our friends and families, who often had no idea where we were or what was happening. I didn't have kids then so it didn't resonate in the way it would now, but some of the crew had left their families for six weeks. Everyone took it in turns to be ill and, at one point, Eric caught dengue fever, which is really serious. I mentioned the catalogue of disaster on our live BBC *Breakfast* chat and didn't think about the impact it would have on everyone's families back at home. We had to put out some reassuring messages that all was OK.

The maximum time I could take off from *Blue Peter* was six weeks and I had to paddle 2,010 miles, so I worked out that would be seventy-five miles a day. It wasn't how many I COULD do in a day; it was how many I HAD to do to be in with a chance of completing the challenge. One morning, they said, 'Come on Helen, we think you can do eighty-five miles by sundown and set a world record for the furthest a woman has kayaked in a day.' In fact, the truth was they had discovered a town further up the river and were hoping for beer. I was oblivious to this, and paddled harder. I did get the world record and they got their beers. Better still, we saw other people who weren't our boat crew.

It was stupidly hard. In the early days, I was dehydrated and throwing up over myself because I didn't want to lean out over the kayak. The heat was immense. As well as dealing with illness, we got covered in mosquito bites – we counted more than forty on one of Eric's hands – and my poor hands were like corned beef from being in the water every day and holding a paddle. My backside was bruised and blistered from being on a hard plastic seat all day, and paddling all those hours was certainly taking its toll on my arms and shoulders. And yet, we were seeing sights we may never see again and experiencing places some people wait their whole lives to visit. I didn't want to just paddle on autopilot so I reminded myself daily to take it all in. Eric even wrote the Elton John lyric about not wishing it away and remembering it wasn't forever from 'I Guess That's Why They Call It the Blues' on our map. A sentiment that has kept my head in check many, many times over the years since.

There were river dolphins, sloths, scorpions and massive tarantulas. If you were a kid dreaming of a mad Amazonian adventure, then this was it. We would eat fish for supper – including some I had inadvertently caught when they jumped into my kayak. At the narrower parts of the river, we would go past villages with houses on stilts where women washed clothes in the river and kids played. Some had never seen people outside of their own village. On other occasions, people came out and paddled with me! Bizarrely, before we set off, we had been interviewed by South American TV, so occasionally I was recognised and people wanted to join me to show their support. We stopped in Manaus to go to the carnival in fancy dress and that felt surreal after being in a kayak all day. These were some of the loveliest moments of the trip. Families lived along the river, giving us an insight into a different way of life and reminding us how we take some valuable commodities for granted, like coffee. It was an adventure in every sense of the word: where we would sleep, what we would eat, what might bite us. We even ended up on the back of police motorbikes at one border crossing, when there were concerns about who had the right paperwork. We stocked up on machetes in case pirates boarded the boat to steal our coffee and sugar. My kids love it when I get mine out to cut the occasional birthday cake, although in truth I think I love it more than them.

We were aware of the health and safety rules put in place to protect us, but we had a brilliant guide, Doodoo, who could navigate around what was acceptable and what wasn't. We swam in the river a lot and never encountered piranhas because he knew where and when we could get into the water. I even held a caiman, known to be more aggressive than alligators. There was the occasional scorpion in the bottom of my kayak and tarantula on my bed, but the mosquitos really were the deadliest of all because of the threat of malaria. Those and the river traffic. I would paddle past enormous freight ships carrying as many as ten articulated lorries. If the river was like a motorway then I was on the equivalent of a tricycle. There was one hairy moment when a ship loomed in my path. Eric contacted them on the radio to tell them to steer clear, saying, 'History is about to be made by this girl from *Blue Peter* who is paddling the length of the Amazon!' It was clear that the captain of the ship couldn't give a toss. He was just doing his job and we were in his way so he kept sounding his horn and shouting at us to move, which was fair enough.

I will never forget the sights and sounds of the Amazon or the feeling of being low in the water and looking at the river and the sky for days on end. I don't think I truly appreciated the strength I got from being in nature back then. Now I realise that when I am in those environments it feels like coming home. I know that sounds strange because it was a foreign place to me and unlike anywhere I had ever been, but I got comfort and confidence from being surrounded by the isolation and unpredictability of the natural world. In that sense, it reminded me of the place I grew up in. Sometimes, I would sit in my little kayak and watch the sky changing, the clouds gathering and a storm rolling up the river towards us. There was that smell you get moments before a storm breaks, followed by raindrops the size of pebbles and a wind that could push you back up the river. It was brutal so there was no point in me trying to paddle. I would be forced off the water, stressed that it was delaying me but humbled by the lack of control in the face of nature. Some greater force was laughing at my seventy-five-mile-a-day schedule. Instead,

I would join the crew on the big boat. Once, Lucy, the doctor, put on her bikini and danced around in the rain, relieved to be in clean, cold water.

The team embraced it all, knowing how lucky we were to experience something that most people don't have the opportunity to do in their lifetimes. Gav would say, 'This is as good as it gets, am I right?!' It was a rhetorical question because he knew what our answer would be. Yes, there were many difficult times. There was illness, dehydration and terrible weather. There was the time the police boarded the boat because several of the crew didn't have the right injections and passport stamps. And, once, the boat started sinking (it was fine in the end and we managed to repair it). There were definitely times when the tears fell, as big as Amazonian raindrops, and this was caught on film forever, but if I think about that time now, it just seems amazing.

Plenty of people have discounted my efforts because they feel it was just for the cameras. It's true that a camera crew brings a level of support, praise and safety that most people don't get. I know that. It's why I don't like to be called an adventurer because I am not. I am a broadcaster who has made telly programmes about adventuring. It's a very different thing and I never confuse the two. If something goes wrong, I have a crew there to get me out of it. I understand that. The caveat to this is that in making good television, I have to put myself in physically and emotionally vulnerable situations and tell people how bad I feel. These are not always emotional threads you want to pull on in front of the nation, but sometimes you have no guard left. I have always tried to take the audience with me and shared a lot of the struggle. It has got harder the longer I am in the telly game, as my profile grows and I have children who will watch me. The consequences of my openness back then have a personal impact now.

The Amazon River empties into the Atlantic Ocean, which wasn't a practical place for us to use as an end point, so instead we chose a town as close to the end as we could. The last couple of days, when we knew we were going to make it, we made sure we enjoyed every second. I had been using a map throughout the journey but I couldn't bring myself to open it out fully to see how ridiculously far I had to paddle. Instead, I would unfold a section at a time and at the end of each day, I would colour in the bit I had just travelled. It was a technique I had used when I was running the ultra-marathon in Namibia and it really helped to break up the challenge into manageable chunks. In the kayak, I would reset my GPS every sixteen miles because that was a distance I could mentally cope with, and once I had hit my target for the day, the crew would play a song over the radio, like Michael Jackson's 'Heal the World'. I couldn't wait to open out the map completely and see just how far I had come.

After 2,018 miles we finished to what was reported as gunfire. It turned out to be fireworks but everyone back at home thought we had been ambushed for a moment. I paddled into the record books too, becoming the first woman to solo kayak the length of the Amazon River.

A few months after I had returned from the trip, I was filming somewhere and this bloke came up to me. He linked my arm and thanked me for doing the adventure. He said he watched me on BBC *Breakfast* every Saturday morning while he was having chemotherapy and radiotherapy, and I had got him through it because as he was battling with his challenge, so was I. He said he felt like we were in the fight together and he didn't want to let me down by giving up on his treatment. I thought, *What an incredible privilege to be in this man's life and be able to help in some way without even knowing it.* That man and that chat have stayed with me and always will.

I can't leave this chapter without writing about my cousin Kate, as she had big plans to visit the Amazon too. She didn't get the chance because she was killed in a road accident. I had been away in Italy with *Blue Peter* filming with the boys, drinking Aperol and taking gondolas down canals. I returned on a high and got a call from my parents to say I needed to come home immediately. It was devastating for our entire family on Dad's side. Kate was a year older than me and we grew up together so were very close. I had also lost another cousin, Sharon, on Mum's side, who died of breast cancer. It was unfathomable to me that these two wonderful young people had been taken away too soon and they became the reason I lean into every birthday and milestone. I don't take anything for granted.

From when she was a small child, Kate was utterly selfless and wanted to change the world. She was an environmental scientist and had just finished her PhD. The day we lost her, she was on her way to help someone else finish theirs. It isn't my tragedy to talk about because it involves the rest of my family, but what I can say is how much losing her and witnessing other people's grief impacted me. Kate's work was dedicated to discovering more about the destruction of the ozone layer and she had planned to go to the Amazon for research purposes. Instead, by total coincidence, I was there and I thought of her as I paddled. She would have loved it. I smile when I hear people talk about the issues surrounding fast fashion and sustainability, fair trade and legacies. She knew about all of that stuff before it was high on the agenda. Her attitudes, even as a teenager, will forever be an example I aspire to follow.

9

Don't Look Down

'By the time I was standing at the top of Battersea Power Station I should have known exactly what I was doing, but I was an absolute wreck.'

I had mixed emotions about returning to normal life after six weeks on the Amazon River. Even wearing shoes and walking on pavements felt weird. As hard as it had been, my life there had been about doing the miles every day, day after day, and nothing else mattered. Luckily, I came back to a flurry of media excitement, which was a good distraction. Sharing stories about my Amazon experience stopped me from missing it too badly and when Comic Relief asked me if I was up for doing more, I jumped at the opportunity. It had made sense to take on an endurance challenge for Sport Relief but Comic Relief needed a different approach.

I had watched *Man on Wire,* about a high-wire walker, on a flight to Sierra Leone and I'd thought it looked cool. So why not have a go?! After much debate and research, we settled on Battersea Power Station as the place for the ultimate challenge. We had talked to HSBC about walking between high-rise buildings at Canary Wharf but, funnily enough, an international bank didn't want to get involved in such a mad idea. We talked about Cheddar Gorge, but it was hard to know if this would have enough of an impact. So Jane, the production manager, managed to persuade the owners of Battersea Power Station that we should do it there. This was back in the day when the power station was still a derelict building. The plan was for me to walk from one of the chimneys on the river side across to the other, south towards Battersea.

There was no real time to think about the task ahead. I was filming, enjoying London as a twenty-something single girl, still on a high after the Amazon and I had the wind in my sails. It was only when I got to France, the place where all my training would take place, that I realised what lay in store. I was being coached by Jade and Karine Kindar-Martin, who had met in Cirque de Soleil. He walked on high wires; she did stunts. They were beautiful and talented, with a young family and a small-holding in France. They welcomed me into their home, their family and their unusual profession.

As gorgeous as the setting and the family were, there was no getting away from the intensity of the situation. Real high-wire walkers risk death when they do their thing, so no one was taking this lightly. And, as much as I was doing kids' TV, I learned quickly not to disrespect the wire or the art. It's always hard when television types meet people who are the best in their field and call the shots. There are parts of each world which don't always co-exist easily and I often find myself in the middle. Jade remains a master of his art and I always look out for his name, Karine's, or their children's in the stunt section of film credits.

I went to France several times – a week here, a few days there. I was trying to get my head around the idea I had to walk on a wire the same thickness as ten-pence pieces over a hundred metres in the air. I had to be able to balance while holding a 12kg pole several metres in length that was supposed to help me. I learned how to walk back and forth and then Jade taught me more tricks, like how to sit down, stand up and salute. It was not something I found easy. For practice, I attempted tight-rope-walking in a tutu with a circus in London's Hyde Park, but it was a totally different skill. I had no pole and the line was much tighter than I was used to so it ended with me being booed. I was seriously intimidated.

Jade would make me stand on the wire for ages, practising how to balance before he would let me take any steps. I would fall and land one leg either side of the taut metal 'wire', which in practice was a pole. The bruises on my arms and undercarriage were horrendous. He wanted me to learn like real high-wire walkers and so I fell, I scrambled, I cried and I pulled myself up ont o that wire. Time after time after time. Often, I was left dangling in the harness, humiliated and exhausted, as I tried, failed and occasionally managed to get back onto the wire. It was a little bit *Rocky* and a little bit *Karate Kid*.

By the time I was standing at the top of Battersea Power Station I should have known exactly what I was doing, but I was an absolute wreck. The *Blue Peter* team had come from BBC TV Centre to cheer me on; my friends were watching from a boat on the Thames; there was a large group of school children and they stopped the overground train so all the passengers got to see too.

I remember the faff and the fuss. There was make-up. A costume. Sound men attaching microphones. There were representatives from Comic Relief and bigwigs from the BBC. The weather was horrible – the wind howled and rain came in sideways. I was so terrified. I remember standing on the scaffolding and the team who had rigged the wire were feeling nervous too. Battersea Power Station was derelict then and I was surrounded by dead pigeons and broken scaffolding, which made it feel like the scene of a bad guy's lair in a film. I just wanted to get on with it, but the weather was slowing us down.

I stood on the top of the scaffolding with a hundred-plus metres of wire in front of me and tried to remember the health and safety talk of what to do should the towers fall. I could hear the distant shout of a crowd of kids chanting 'Helen! Helen! Helen!' In France, I'd had gorgeous greenery slowly falling away underneath me. Here, I had a sheer drop, a concrete pillar and then nothing but that wire. I was given an earpiece so the producer could talk to me and remind me to breathe. Three steps, then breathe. The same again. Again and again. When I ran the eighty miles in Namibia, in my head I only ever ran five miles lots of times. I knew I could run five miles so I did that, again and again. In the Amazon, as I said, I knew I could kayak sixteen miles, so I only ever thought about doing that before repeating it, many times over. On this wire, all I had to do was take three steps and then another three. Sliding one foot over the other and keeping as much of my feet in contact with the wire as possible.

Jade wasn't flustered; he was matter of fact. 'What's the aim of the game?' he asked. To which I replied, 'To stay on the wire!' Without taking my eyes off it, I stepped out, fingers clenched around the pole, my feet gripping the wire beneath my feet, and began. I took a breath every third step. The wind and my lack of nerve made the wire quiver and I knew I needed to take control. Just like when I wobbled on the skateboard. It was the same here as my fears were shaking out of my body and making it harder. Jade could see how nervous I was but he was pleased I was using the techniques he had taught me. Halfway along the wire the wind really picked up and I felt completely exposed. The towers were fragile so the wire had to be rigged in a certain way, which meant it dipped in the middle. As the uphill got steeper in the second half, my arms were burning with the weight of the pole. I knew I was almost there but I didn't dare look up. I got to the platform and screamed with relief as everyone watching cheered and the guy who'd set up the wire actually jumped with joy. To this day, watching his reaction gives me goosebumps and it feels like an honour to do a job that makes people react like that.

Jade was happy for me, although mildly disappointed. He wanted to know why I hadn't done any of the tricks he had taught me. I should have sat down or done the salute. But I was too scared and I didn't want to showboat and risk losing lose my balance. I told him the challenge was to walk across the wire and that was what I did. I needed to control my fear much more than I needed to prove I could salute.

People asked, why do it, if you were so scared? I said that I didn't want to let anyone down. On this challenge, I could feel the power of the team because I was on home turf and I could see the support and reaction first-hand. Jane had worked hard to persuade the owners of the power station to let us put up a wire so some girl could try to walk across it. That's not an easy conversation to have and that was not lost on me. I am very aware that I got all the glory for the challenges I took on but there were a lot of people behind the scenes who made them happen. The least I could do was walk out onto the wire. It's about being part of a team and I think that is relevant in everything I have done.

10

Comic Relief

*'I got thanked for bringing the comedy element and
I genuinely wasn't trying to be funny.'*

I have been part of the wonderful Comic Relief family for a
big part of my career. From filming on a Rio rubbish dump
and visiting vulnerable children in Uganda to kayaking down
the Amazon and cycling to the South Pole, I have taken
on incredible, emotional and sometimes almost impossible
tasks and loved every minute of it. The teams behind Comic
Relief and Sport Relief are fantastic and I would do (almost)
anything they ask of me. I can't think of a better way to
raise funds and awareness than the way they do – through
storytelling, sharing hard-hitting facts, involving high-profile

people and entertaining the audience. They are a national treasure.

As well as the big, meaty projects I was involved with, I have also been part of smaller but just as important opportunities to help, like taking part in *Let's Dance for Comic Relief, The Great Sport Relief Bake Off* and *Sport Relief Celebrity Boxing.* Each of these programmes reminded me who I was or taught me things about myself I didn't know. Including, in one memorable case, that I shouldn't ever bake a cake again.

My first experience of working for Comic Relief was in 2009. I was in the middle of pinging around the country and the world, filming an eclectic and sometimes bizarre mix of stuff for *Blue Peter,* when I was invited to take part in *Let's Dance.* The producers wanted to put together a dance group of past and present *Blue Peter* presenters and I jumped at the chance to be involved. It was my first experience of the shiny floor multi-camera show and I had my own dressing room and runner. Not something we were used to coming from *Blue Peter,* where I would get changed in a corner of the studio! I also saw the juggernaut of hair, make-up and wardrobe at full throttle and something inside me lit up.

Our group consisted of Anthea Turner, Janet Ellis, Tim Vincent, Mark Curry, Diane-Louise Jordan, Peter Duncan and little old me. I had met the women before at the big photo-shoot we had done. It was lovely to be reunited with them and by now I had a little more experience of the industry so didn't feel as intimidated as I had when we first met. Our dance was to Elvis Presley's 'Jailhouse Rock'. We were on the same night as Paddy McGuinness and Keith Lemon, who performed '(I've Had) The Time of My Life' from *Dirty Dancing*, and Jo Brand, who was transformed into Britney Spears. They were fabulous. This first dip into showbusiness was a revelation to me. After being convinced I was going to be a news reporter, I saw how easily I was seduced by a bit of sparkle.

Five years later, I took part in *The Great Sport Relief Bake Off*. I went into it to have a nice time and be around fun people. I did not think about the actual baking required. I underestimated how seriously everyone would take it and quickly realised I was out of my depth. My fellow contestants Rochelle Humes, Doon Mackichan and Alistair McGowan were streets ahead of me. Let's put it this way: I got thanked for bringing the comedy element and I genuinely wasn't trying to be funny.

When I arrived, I sat down in the make-up chair and they said, 'Oh, we are Rochelle's team!' At first I just said, 'OK, cool,' because I didn't get what they meant. Then I said, 'Oh shit, do you mean get out of the chair?' I hadn't realised they were there exclusively for her. Not the first nor the last time I have put my foot in it or been in the wrong place. It continued as it had started, with me a few steps behind everyone else and being laughed at. In a nice way, of course. Even though I had done quite a bit of telly by this point, I had come from a *Blue Peter* background of mucking in so my feet were firmly on the ground. I wasn't used to hair and make-up teams, catering or dressing rooms, but I was very happy to be surrounded by them. It made me realise how much I liked telly and my job. How much every bit, no matter how tiny, is taken so seriously. Few people do things half-heartedly in telly and tiredness isn't really an option.

I thought if I did *Bake Off*, I could prove to my family and friends that I wasn't useless in the kitchen. When I was at school, I made an apple crumble and after forty minutes I couldn't understand why it was still cold. It turned out I had put the oven light on, not the heat.

When I lived with long-suffering Rebecca in London, we didn't cook. When I say we didn't cook, we really didn't cook anything ever. We lived together for a few years and when she left to move in with her boyfriend, Chris, we had a leaving party. Chris said, 'Let's cook something for the party.' He opened the cooker and the plastic wrapping was still in there. He couldn't believe we hadn't used the oven for the entire time we were there, but we were at a different stage in life. We wanted to be out on the town talking to bankers in moleskin trousers rather than rustling up a lasagne. I suggested making a big batch of

My dad, the most selfless, good man I know.
He makes a mean pancake.

Me and my Big Bro in the farm house
we grew up in.

As a kid, I was never far from
a farm pup, a stray cat,
or a broken bird.

I have always been happiest outside, and happiest on the move.
My brother has always been happiest with a football at his feet.

I played every sport at school,
including hockey with two of my
besties Shellie and Kim.

My school friends are still
my best friends. Here's me
wearing a scarf fashioned
as a top on a night out
with Rebecca and Kim.

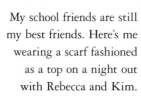

One of our *Blue Peter* summer trips, this time to Italy. Joel, Ayo, and I travelled north to south at one point delivering pizzas on vintage Vespas.

Crossing the line after running seventy-eight miles in the Namibian desert with ten minutes left on the clock.

Blisters galore. Thank goodness Lucy, the doctor, taped me up constantly before I set off, meaning I could paddle for up to sixteen hours a day and keep the blisters under control.

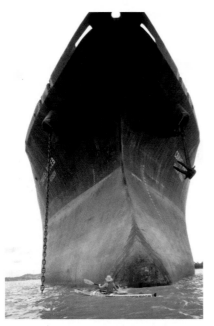

The other boats on the water were pretty big.

Carrying on the kayaking with my boys.

Crewmates Gav, Eric and Stu. The best adventure with the best people.

On the farm filming for Christmas whilst I was nine months pregnant with Elsie. Jules and JB offered to help should anything happen. I said I wanted one of the vets.

There's often a goat climbing on me, a donkey biting me or a cow licking me. One of the many reasons I love this show.

The programmes I am most proud of are the *Blue Peter* appeal films. Here, I was drawing with children waiting for cleft lip operations.

In Sierra Leone, I met children who walked miles for water and lost family due to poor sanitation.

Walking a high wire between the chimneys at Battersea power station.

A true exercise in finding balance.

Cycling, kite-skiing, and walking to the South Pole in 2012, our smiles frozen stiff as we set a world record.

Some of the crew whose logistics we were tagging on to. Setting up camps in minus seventy-degree temperatures and fifty miles per hour wind definitely tests your friendship!

At the Rio Olympics, 2016, watching British athletes prove Britain is good at swimming and diving. Adam Peaty set the place on fire.

In Budapest in 2017. Working with Mark Foster and Becky Adlington is a gift. Hilarious, talented, and a joy to be around.

Becoming a mum.
Louis was born in 2017 in the
kitchen in France, delivered
by my wonderful friend Jill,
who even took this beautiful
photo despite all the chaos.

Snuggling Ernie, we moved to the south
of France when he was a few months old.
He learned to walk on this beach.

Wining and dining with my gorgeous girl.
She steals hearts wherever she goes.

chilli for the party, having never made it before. Luckily for all our guests, I didn't get round to it. To this day, it remains a running joke. When I plan to meet up with Rebecca and Chris, he says to Rebecca, 'Get Helen to make a chilli.' I still haven't made one. Maybe that's why neither Rebecca nor I begrudge our nights of fish fingers and beans on toast or miss cocktails in Soho. We had a good time at the right time and now we have six children between us. I actually enjoy freezer Fridays when I get the fish fingers out.

I thought I would be told what to cook on *Bake Off*, like I was on *Blue Peter,* and I didn't realise I had to turn up with recipes or even, heaven forbid, have practised beforehand. This was still in the early days of the show, so I didn't know that much about it. I had various cooking catastrophes, including dropping my Eccles cakes and then lying about it. I was asked several times if I had dropped the cake that I was just about to give to the classy and elegant Mary Berry. Mary was not yet a dame at that point but it was obvious she should be made one pretty damn quick. I continued to deny dropping the cakes. Absolutely not! Unfortunately, I had not banked on what felt like fifty cameras recording my every move so I had to come clean, but I told them it was OK because I had brushed them off and employed the ten-second floor rule.

We also made pizzas and Paul Hollywood was horrified to see I had put halloumi on mine. He said it was a big mistake and I argued that it was subjective and depended on what you liked to eat. This was a high-level faux pas because I shouldn't be telling a judge and master baker how to cook, apparently. He pulled the same confused face when I told him I didn't have my own celebrity calendar, so couldn't empathise with how embarrassing he found it when his parents made him sign his calendars for their friends. I said, 'Paul, at no point ever am I going to have a calendar and if I did, I am pretty sure my parents wouldn't be giving it to their friends!' He's got such a hypnotising face. It's the eyes – they're like a Siberian husky's. Lovely man. Lovely eyes.

We had to make a sporting-themed cake and mine began to go wrong very quickly. No matter, I could solve the issues by covering it with icing. Which I did – one inch in some places and seven inches in others. It was supposed to be a mountain with marzipan skiers bombing down it to represent my Antarctic adventures, but my figures were so terrible that I just made the legs and the skis and stuck them upside down in the icing to make it look like they had crashed.

When it came to the judges' chat at the end to decide who was going to win, Paul and Mary said, 'Well, obviously we are going to eliminate Helen.' And Ed Byrne, who was hosting, said, 'Blimey, that's a bit mean, isn't it? Just because she's shit at baking you don't need to eliminate her!' It sounded like they were going to do away with me!

I am still terrible in the kitchen. I don't have the patience or the organisation for baking. I cook because I have to feed the kids, not because I like it. It is not a hobby or a stress reliever. When I invite friends round for dinner, it's not uncommon for them to bring their own food. If I was super rich, I would have a chef for sure. And I would get them to put halloumi on my pizzas.

Sport Relief Celebrity Boxing came along in 2018 at the perfect time. I was married to the Rugby League player Richie Myler (I'll tell you the story of how we met a little later on!) , and we had been living in the South of France, where he had been playing rugby until he accepted an offer from a Leeds club. We returned when Ernie was two and Louis was ten months, so I wasn't quite ready to take on any big projects or sign up for work that would take me away from them. Settling into Leeds took some time after two years living in what was essentially a holiday resort in the South of France. I really missed the lifestyle and the friends I had made there. Yes, we were coming home to England, but moving to a new city with tiny children can feel like moving to a foreign country because we didn't have NCT or baby-group friends, nor did we have family or friends anywhere near. I didn't know anyone and I didn't really know city life. Although I had lived in Manchester and London, I had done so as a young, single, working woman, and moving to a new city with two small children is a different prospect. It was a strange transition period which would have felt pretty bleak without a punchbag to take my stress out on.

I signed up for the boxing competition because I can't resist an invitation from Sport Relief. I thought this would be a great way to get fit, have a laugh and raise money for charity. What I didn't bank on was finding a pal in the process. Phil Sellers, my boxing coach, was also my saviour. He was the most unlikely friend at one of the weirdest times in my life and I told him so. I bet it would be hard to count how many lost souls he has helped over the years. I know he was sceptical at first about training a TV presenter but I think I won him round.

The training schedule worked with my kids because the sessions were only half an hour long. That said, they were intensive and I sweated buckets throughout. I couldn't keep weight on. I stopped drinking and started looking after myself because I knew how exposing the fight would be and I didn't want to embarrass myself on television. I thought I would enjoy the training but it surprised me how much I also loved the boxing club and all the people I met. The experience reminded me of those boxing films where some guy, down on his luck, finds boxing and a way to a happy life. It feels like this is what the sport is good at, giving people from a certain walk of life something remarkable. I witnessed it first-hand. I used to spar with a girl in Hull. She was in her early twenties with a seven-year-old boy and boxed in the gym most days. She was doing part-time jobs and studying a full-time degree to become a hospital theatre nurse. There wasn't a single second she didn't fill. We bang on about girl power – well, she was the epitome of it. She used to say to me, 'If you don't punch me in the face, you're disrespecting what we do.' I had spent thirty years not punching people in the face but this was not a woman I wanted to disrespect in any way.

The other celebrities taking part were based in London. I was fighting Camilla Thurlow (originally from *Love Island*) and the second match was between Vanessa White (from pop group The Saturdays) and Hannah Spearritt (from pop group S Club 7). They all trained together and went to lots of boxercise classes. I definitely got the grittier experience working with Phil at the hardcore but brilliant Burmantofts Amateur Boxing Club in Leeds.

The club ticked all the stereotypical boxes. Smells of sweat? Yes. Cracked leather punchbags? Absolutely. Boxes of hand wraps? Definitely. Every inch of the wall was covered in photos of young lads in boxing poses. Phil took me through them and I would point and ask, what about him? World Champion. And him? Commonwealth Champion. Some of them didn't have the same success, instead going down darker paths. It's the grittiness and uncertainty that encapsulated the sport to me.

Phil took me under his professional wing and was determined to make a boxer out of me. It was brutal too. I had to train with someone who was the same weight as me, so I worked with a female Commonwealth champion in Bradford, and some of the girls in the GB squad in Sheffield let me join them in the ring a few times. These girls were at the top of their game and the environment was intense. They were lean and tough and made me feel sluggish just looking at them as they bounced from toe to toe and danced around the ring. They would throw a punch from nowhere that would leave me staggering. I even broke a tooth in one spar. I took a blow to the nose that was so hard I thought I would pass out, but Phil just said, 'Unless you can smell mustard, you haven't been hit hard enough.' I have never been a fighter, or even had much of a temper, but something about someone boxing you on the nose makes you want to retaliate. It's an odd feeling. You don't want to throw a punch, you feel awkward, then someone swings for you and you're like 'OK LET'S GO!' Those girls coaxed me into it.

By comparison, I also joined a training session for amateur boxers preparing to fight in what's termed a white-collar boxing match, where white-collar professionals train to fight at special events, likely with no prior experience. Now, that was awful. I could smell sweat and blood as soon as I walked up the concrete stairs of the gym, housed in a warehouse in a part of Leeds I was pretty scared of. Some of the women took one look at me and smirked. Everyone wanted to knock my block off and they weren't shy about telling me they would. The only thing stopping me running for the door was the group of kickboxers between me and the exit. I genuinely couldn't get out. So we sparred. I took a few hits to the head, ducked a few, thanked everyone and legged it to my car for a good private cry.

This was a level of fitness I had never known before or since. I trained hard. Being pummelled in the ring for three or four rounds of two-minute action was one of the most tiring things I have ever done. Phil and another coach, John, had taken me to watch some amateur fights and had put me in some gut-wrenchingly intimidating environments, so I knew I was battle ready. Or, at least, I felt it by the time the TV fight came around. I'd lost a tooth, I'd smelt mustard . . . it was time.

On the night of the fight, I felt good. I didn't know how the other girls had got on in training. I knew nothing about boxing, but I knew Phil was the best trainer I could have wished for. We had dinner the night before and Wayne Bridge, one of the other boxers, listed some of my other adventures and said to my opponent's coach, 'Good luck to whoever is boxing Helen.' Phil just winked. The mind games were full throttle.

After all the practice I had been put through, I was more than ready for the contest. I had been in rough gyms with rough people who were very open about wanting to knock me out and then trying to. I had to channel it all into this moment and persuade my brain that it was OK to hit my beautiful opponent in the face.

I was introduced as Helen 'The Hellraiser' Skelton and boxed my way over to the ring, waiting for Camilla 'The Thunderbolt' Thurlow. The match started and the two of us boxed three rounds. Phil had always said that as soon as the whistle goes, go all out for the first punch and set the intent. I did that. And then some. I was lucky that I was on the front foot and I was taller than Camilla. I had the experience of being on the receiving end of some brutal blows so I was ready. I did get a couple of stoppages and the ref asked me to calm down. I have a lot of respect for Camilla and anyone who gets in a ring like that, so it was a weird victory. As an amateur, I hope I did the sport justice and didn't come across as a telly type having a half-hearted go.

Ore Oduba interviewed us in the ring afterwards and asked if I had a message for my family and friends who were there to support me. I could see Richie in the audience and so I said, 'Babe, did you put a wash on before you came out?!' I loved making a joke of our switch in role and felt that buzz of girl power. Richie thought it was hilarious and said how proud he was of me.

Afterwards, the referee came up to me and encouraged me to continue boxing in the future but I knew I was done. I had achieved what I set out to do. I said to Phil I was going to retire undefeated immediately!

As much as I loved training with Phil, I hope he also enjoyed spending time with me and appreciated the work I put in. I know he thought I was mentally strong and wanted to win, which was half the battle. I didn't need praise, just to keep being pushed and this was exactly what he did. It's now a joke at Radio 5 Live that I will mention boxing within an hour of being on the radio, but that's because it was one of the most incredible things I ever did. So, never let it be said that I am underprepared for a challenge! Anything I take on gets my full attention and commitment and I want to achieve it to the best of my ability – unless it's baking a batch of fairy cakes.

I can't leave this chapter without sharing the funniest postscript to my Comic Relief career. I went to Number Ten for a Comic Relief reception and I met this woman who was cool and sassy and exactly the sort of woman I wanted to be. We chatted and she told me her daughter had curvature of the spine and needed a lot of operations. I was sorry to hear this and she invited me to call in to their house and see her if I had time. I said I would. I was a *Blue Peter* presenter so I was used to being asked to do this kind of thing, and I was only too happy to. The nice lady gave me her address.

I rocked up to this incredible house in west London and thought, *Oh, I wonder what they do*. I met the woman's daughter,

Scarlett, a super-intelligent, incredible young woman who was coping with major surgery in a truly remarkable way. When I walked down the stairs there were lots of family photos on the wall and Lenny Henry was in one of them. Stella McCartney was in another one. And I thought, *Aye up, who are these people?!* All I knew was I had met an amazing woman whose just as amazing daughter was having a rough time, and, for some reason, her mum said she may get a little boost from my visit. In truth, Scarlett gave me a boost and to this day I am in awe of her. But it had dawned on me that this wasn't a normal family. Then Scarlett's dad came in and said, 'Sorry, we've got to go now because we are popping over to *The X Factor* to see my friend Simon.' Now, that was a big clue.

Once I left, I did a bit of digging and discovered the nice lady was Emma Freud and her partner, Scarlett's dad, was Richard Curtis. The same duo who'd founded and run Comic Relief and Sport Relief. Oh my golly goodness. I had absolutely no idea.

It wasn't just me. My mum made the same faux pas when I was walking the high wire. Several people from Comic Relief had come down to watch. My parents were there too. It was a building site at the time so everyone was wearing hard hats stamped with the logo of the construction company, Balfour Beatty. There was a buzz that someone important was about to arrive and my mum was introduced to him. 'Here he is,' someone said, 'You know who this is, don't you?!' And Mum said, 'Of course I do, it's Mr Balfour Beatty, says so on his hat.' There was sharp intake of breath from all the big cheeses. It was Richard Curtis. Of course, Mum knew who he was, but she didn't know what he looked like.

It's testament to Richard that, as a film director and charity founder, neither of us recognised him. He is not front and centre scooping the accolades, he is working hard behind the scenes, as is his partner, Emma, who champions others with such magical energy and enthusiasm. She's a woman's woman and I am a big fan. I could fill this book with encounters like that. Sometimes London is a bit of a bubble for famous people. I have never been very good at knowing the people I 'should' be talking to and I am not interested in who is in the boardroom. When I met the old controller of BBC One about future work possibilities, I spent the entire meeting talking to him about sport and my dad's job, working with artificial insemination. There was a tennis ball in his office and I kept bouncing it and throwing it in the air. When I left I thought, *Yep, pretty sure I just wasted that opportunity.* I had just told the big boss about bull sperm.

Recently, I was back at the BBC for a meeting. I went to reception, said who I was meeting and gave my name. The receptionist misheard Skelton and rang him, saying, 'I have Helen, your girlfriend, here to see you.' In the lift I thought,

This will be funny! It's a good ice-breaker. But by the time I got there, he was sweating, and he did the entire meeting sitting on the threshold of the room with his foot outside the door. It's remarkable that I am still in this industry.

11

Cycling to the South Pole

*'Looking after the little things often means
the bigger things look after themselves.'*

It was the one hundredth anniversary of the two explorers, the
Norwegian, Roald Amundsen, and the Brit, Robert Falcon
Scott, racing to reach the South Pole in 1911. What better way
to celebrate their achievement and raise money for Sport Relief
than for me to follow in their legendary footsteps? Yet again,
it took some persuading for the BBC bosses to consider it. It
was costly, involved huge risk and would take me and the crew
away for a big chunk of time. What swung it was the decision
to make a separate six-episode series, a *Blue Peter* spin-off. As
thrilled as I was, I was concerned about how interesting it would

be for the viewers if I walked the route twelve hours a day with my furry hood up. We needed to be a bit more creative.

The stakes were higher this time around. I now had a reputation for taking on impossible adventures, while there were also other better-known people, such as James Cracknell and Ben Fogle, undertaking tough challenges. In telly, the mood was shifting and the focus, quite rightly, was on justifying these expeditions because of the financial and environmental impacts. Plus, it was dangerous. There is a reason why fewer people have been to the South Pole than have walked up Everest. Also, around this time, *Blue Peter* moved to Salford, which was hard for some of the team because they loved working on the programme but didn't want to relocate. So it was stressful for the show. In the midst of it all, I decided I was going to get to the South Pole by bicycle and kite skis.

I was well aware how ridiculous it sounded to take a bicycle to the Antarctic. But I also knew that we had to catch the nation's attention. For those of you wondering what it is like to cycle in snow . . . well, imagine cycling on sand. The training schedule was epic. I started around five months before the expedition, which stressed one of the researchers who said some people train exclusively for a couple of years. I went to California to learn how to use a sand bike, to New Zealand to learn how to kite-ski, and to Iceland and Greenland for cold-weather training. In Iceland, we had to be rescued off the mountain in a terrible storm and spent the night in a little bothy. That was just the training course. It was exciting, dramatic and right up my street.

Even better, I got to meet and film with the British explorer and writer, Sir Ranulph Fiennes. He had completed incredible expeditions over the years and was the first to cross the Antarctic without support. What an amazing man! I went to his house and we got on immediately. He told me the story of returning from the North Pole with terrible frostbite in the fingers on one hand and his surgeon instructing him to wait before amputation. The pain was too great so he sawed his fingers off and showed me the desk where he did it, along with the hacksaw he used. He then put me through my training paces in his back garden, commanding me to drag a heavy sled and then get up on a sandbank with it. If Sir Ranulph asks you to do something then you do it, so I did.

When I got back he was crying with laughter: 'I said that as a joke! I didn't think you were actually going to do it! But then I watched you and I thought, if she gets up there she will be fine!' And I was. I loved meeting him; he is an absolute legend. Though it was funny, as polar explorers from other countries who I filmed with couldn't understand our obsession with him. They said, 'Only the British would celebrate a man who ballsed up his expedition to the point where he had to cut his own fingers off. You guys think that's a win?!' An American woman said to me, 'In my country, if we go on a trip and end up missing a few fingers, it's gone wrong.' But we think he is a hero, and he is.

I was paired up with Norwegian kite-skier Niklas Norman, who was a proper adventurer, to accompany me throughout the challenge. He had different expectations and wanted to kite-ski across the entire continent – an impressive challenge which, to this day, has not been achieved He was right with regards to the adventuring but I knew that wouldn't work. It would look like I was on an extreme sports holiday and that does not great television make. Nobody wants to see me travelling by kite ski to the South Pole at seventy miles an hour with a backdrop of blue skies and bright sun. Also, I needed to bicycle too, after spending weeks training and filming it in California. It was difficult for a telly presenter to explain this to a hardened adventurer. We wanted to take very different approaches.

We flew to Cape Town and from there we were going to fly to Antarctica. We had to wait for an appropriate weather window, which I assumed would take a few days maximum but we ended up waiting for ten impatient days. After spending months jumping through all the hoops to be ready for this big adventure, we were at the mercy of the elements. There was a brief moment and we grabbed it, taking a strange plane with no windows flown by Russian pilots, who had a quick shot of vodka before they set off. The rest of the passengers were scientists, who were dropped at various science bases, and a few marines and Norwegians, who were doing what we were doing and heading to the South Pole. We landed at the coast and camped there for a few days before a small plane flew us to the beginning of our 500-mile trek on kite-skis, cross-country skis and an ice bike. Time to set off.

We were tagging a race that was already organised so we piggybacked on to their logistics. The landscape was stunning and brutal. It was wall-to-wall white with twenty-four hours of sunshine and temperatures as low as -48°C. It's also the windiest place on Earth (if that isn't a true fact, then it should be),w hich made it hard to ski or stand up at times, let alone set up a tent. There were no sunrises and sunsets. No golden hour. No shadows. Just white. It was unlike anywhere I had ever been. That sort of thing messes with your head and your body clock and makes survival harder. Where else can you get sunburn and frostbite at the same time? One of the Norwegian team got snow blindness so he was tied to his mate for the duration of the trip. I felt the sheer danger of my environment and the necessity of respecting my training and my support team. Niklas was the expedition leader and planned out our adventure including our kit. I trusted him completely.

After the Amazon – where I had kayaked alone but eaten and slept in the support boat – the producer in Antarctica wanted to push it further. This time, I was separate from the film crew and they were strictly onlookers only, charting my progress.

I had my own tent, which I had to put up and take down every day while wearing mittens that made it feel like I was doing everything in thick oven gloves. It was too cold to ever get undressed so if I washed, it was under my thermals. I washed my hair once at a camp, drying it with a makeshift hairdryer constructed from a blowtorch so it didn't freeze. During training, I had been repeatedly warned about the issues that come from the extreme cold. They shared the story of Sir Ranulph cutting his fingers off, of course, and also a story about an adventurer who was in the usual four layers of thermals, leggings, down trousers and waterproofs, but didn't do up the flies on the base layer of his thermals properly. Consequently, he lost the end of his penis to frostbite. This I took with a pinch of salt; it felt like an urban myth being bandied around. However, when I got back from the trip, I was at an event and a chap came up to congratulate me on the expedition. He asked how I found the cold weather training and whether anyone had mentioned the story of the man who lost the end of his penis. 'Yes,' I said, thinking he was going to tell me it wasn't true. 'That was me,' he replied. I did not ask him to prove it.

I'm quite a chaotic, roll-with-the-punches kinda girl but I learned fast how important it was to trust and respect the processes in such a hostile environment. Putting up the tent, taking it down, making sure there was no snow in it, getting my boots on properly, untangling the kite lines . . . if any of these things (and many others) were forgotten or carelessly handled it could cost me dear. Looking after the little things often means the bigger things look after themselves.

This all reminded me of when I met the adventurer and endurance athlete Lowri Morgan. She is an incredible person and a source of huge inspiration to me. She has done a lot of things men haven't done and I asked her how she had achieved so much. Her answer was that she takes care of the simple things. She drinks before she is thirsty, eats before she is hungry, gets warm before she feels cold and puts blister pads on as soon as she can feel the burn. It may mean she has to pause in the middle of a race to take off her socks and put plasters on, which slows her down, but it also means she is more likely to finish the race. When I was in Namibia, the people who set off on the ultra-marathon the quickest didn't finish. The guy who won the race was the one who walked the first marathon. I am always quoting Lowri Morgan to my children and her words were with me in the middle of the whiteness.

I put all the food rations I needed for the entire twenty-day trip on the back of a sledge. It came in at thirteen stone. In camp, the crew would talk to me but we didn't eat together, and, in the mornings, I watched them light their little stove to fry bacon while I made more of the same porridge. We were out there on Christmas Day 2012 and I was feeling very sorry for myself. There had been a snowstorm, my tent was ripped – which was dangerous – and I had a dodgy stomach from existing on rehydrated food. The crew were doing their thing and I was doing mine, and then I heard the zip of my tent go. They had taken pity on me so they pushed a little Christmas present through the gap. It was a microwaveable Christmas pudding. I mean, what the hell?! I didn't even have a hairbrush, let alone any way to cook this pud. It was another one of those 'choke on your Coca-Cola' moments! I didn't know whether to laugh or cry.

Niklas was in the tent next to mine. He was very good at reminding me to enjoy the trip and take it all in, whereas I was on a mission to just get it done. This is a lesson I have learned several times over in the quests I have undertaken. The truth is I found this challenge the hardest and least fun of all those I had taken on. It defined endurance. We had a few changes to the film crew too. There wasn't much to enjoy during the slog of it all. It's one thing taking on a challenge that is tough and scary but if you feel like you are part of a team then it spurs you on. I missed the end-of-day celebrations we had in the Amazon. This felt relentless. One of the things that keeps me going in life is finding the funny side of a situation, and there really wasn't much to laugh about on this one. In difficult situations I often think, *well at least this will make a good story*, but this eluded me in Antarctica.

When we finally reached the South Pole it was with relief

more than exhilaration. Amazingly, not only had we hit our twenty-day target, but we also set a record for being the first to cycle there and a world best for the quickest 100km using kite skis. It felt good to be ending on a high, but I was glad it was over. There was another reason I was ready to go home. I had met someone.

12

Modern Love

'I wanted unpredictability and adventure.
I wanted the bad boy, not the safe choice.'

I had moved to Manchester when *Blue Peter* relocated and was having the time of my life, travelling around the globe for the job I loved and going on dates with people along the way. My friend Kim worked for the owner of Warrington Rugby League club and knew one of the players, Richie Myler, who she said seemed like fun. She thought we would get on well so she gave me his number and we chatted over the phone for a few months while I was jetting around. Then he asked me out. I remember saying I wasn't really interested in a big night because I was tired, but I would come to the cinema if

I didn't have to chat. How rude was that?! Who would even want to take me out? We had a nice evening and I remember thinking, *Oh! This could be a laugh for a while*. Richie was different to other men I had dated. He was interested in all the random stuff I was doing and encouraged me, rather than feeling threatened or bored by it.

It's hard to say if I had a type. I had some met interesting and lovely people. Some were lovelier to me than I was to them, but most were confused by my chaotic work schedule and unimpressed if I flaked out of dinner plans because I had to go and fly with the Red Arrows or have tea with the Prime Minister. Or if I couldn't make the party because I was going dogsledding or making money boxes out of yoghurt pots. Wonderful men came into my life and I probably didn't appreciate them enough. I let them slip through my fingers because I was too busy having a good time and I wasn't ready for anything more. I think timing is important in love. You can meet the right person at the wrong time and vice versa. I was terribly spoilt by a couple of lovely boyfriends. One turned up at *Blue Peter* and said he was whisking me away to Venice the following week and I said, 'I can't, I'm working.' He said most girls would be grateful but I loved my job and I took it seriously; I couldn't just disappear off on holiday when I felt like it and nor did I want to. The same guy sent a bouquet of flowers to a hotel I was staying at when I was away filming and I felt cross and embarrassed. Ryan the sound man said to me, 'Helen, if your reaction to him sending you flowers is to be angry then he isn't the guy for you. Set him free. Not only do you not appreciate him, you are taking the mickey.' I've said it many times: never upset the sound man. They know EVERYTHING.

I once dated a guy who had a Ferrari and a flat in Berkeley Square. There was a moment when he tried to get serious and wanted to know where our relationship was going, but I wasn't ready. It's easy to look back on this with the benefit of hindsight. Even my dad's like, 'Why did you let that one go?!'

I wanted to fly by the seat of my pants. I wanted unpredictability and adventure. I wanted the bad boy, not the safe choice. So when a rugby player covered in tattoos turned up and showed interest in my strange life and embraced my lack of schedule, I fell for him. We hung out for a while together and then I went off to Antarctica. When I came back, Richie moved in with me. We both had the same zest for life. I knew this when we first met and I was off dragon boat racing with friends. Other men had not understood the appeal of paddling a large boat down the river, but Richie thought it sounded like fun. This was someone I could spend a lot of time with and not get bored. I think the stars were aligned.

Richie proposed on a night out in Manchester. We had dinner and then he took me to a penthouse apartment in a smart hotel and asked me to marry him. It was all happening at lightning speed, but he was fun, supportive and wasn't going to clip my wings. It didn't feel like we were 'settling down'. I thought I had found the perfect example of modern love.

The wedding planning went smoothly, other than a hiccup with the dress. It had been made for me but when I tried it on, I didn't like it. So I popped to a wedding dress shop the week before the wedding and pulled something off the rail. I got a dress on Tuesday and we got married on Sunday. Nothing like cutting it fine.

We got married in December 2013, in my local village church where my grandma had been the organist, and then we took over a big house for the reception. The day was very us, full of laughter, food, music and dancing. We all had a really good time.

Being Mrs Myler wasn't going to change me. I'd always been the kind of woman to go off on holiday by myself or grab an opportunity for an adventure with friends. At the beginning of 2014, Richie went to Australia for six weeks for work and I went on a cycling holiday to Cuba with two girlfriends for a fortnight. We got a lot of attention when we arrived because people couldn't believe we were away without men. When they discovered I had only been married a couple of months they were flabbergasted. Why was I not with my husband? They would ask. 'Why should I be?' I responded.

I have an eclectic mix of pals from different walks of life

rather than one big group of friends. Rebecca and Babs were both keen to come to Cuba even though they are polar opposites. Babs is a doer, a mountain-climber, a marathon-runner and an adventure-lover, the kind of girl to get married in a suit and flip-flops. She has the most beautiful soul. She and I arrived in Cuba with the bare minimum in our backpacks. Rebecca – God love her – had packed her hair extensions and wedge heels. Babs and I were in it for the cycling and planned to cover up to one hundred miles a day, whereas Rebecca wanted to know when we were going to the beach. Initially, our expectations didn't match up and the holiday was at risk of being ruined by the stress and drama this caused. In the end, Rebecca asked each day, 'Where are you cycling to, girls?' We would point to a place on a map and she would put her bike in a taxi and meet us there so we could all hang out.

Cuba wasn't a natural place to cycle around. There was the occasional hardcore cyclist but we were quite the talking point. In the towns, not only would people question why we were three women alone, but also why we were on bikes and not doing the tourist route. The hangover from the Cold War was evident wherever we went, particularly because we were venturing off the typical path. There were limited provisions in the shops and we cycled around behind large American cars. Drivers would beep their horns and think we were mad to be cycling when we could clearly afford a car. Despite the occasional intensity of the trip, we didn't have any problems. We stayed at family B&Bs and they would phone ahead and book us into the next one so we had to trust them. We were never let down or experienced any issues. Havana certainly had an edgy atmosphere, but we had some mad nights out, meeting random people and dancing in the streets. The setting made it feel like we were in a film.

I left *Blue Peter* after five amazing years. It had been the best job in the world but life was changing. I wanted to share some adventures with Richie too. I couldn't do that and be available seven days a week, twenty-four hours a day. After filming at the World Worm Charming Championship, where I was dressed as a chicken, attempting to get worms out of the ground, I thought it may be time to move on. No disrespect to the event, but I had been given some amazing once-in-a-lifetime opportunities, and the disparity between the extreme and surreal challenges was beginning to grate.

Part of the success of *Blue Peter* comes down to being curious about everything. I didn't want to be that person who had stopped appreciating every aspect of the job and enjoying it for what it was. I am still like this now. I want to focus on the things I can give my all to – to keep energy levels high, bring solutions not problems and be a joy to work with. I know what a privileged position I am in and there are many people who want to do my job. When people ask me about professional ambitions, I always say my goal is to do work I enjoy and be grateful to be there. No one wants a presenter rolling their eyes in a chicken costume. Besides, being married felt like a new chapter. I wanted to give more time to my personal life and explore other possibilities in television. Then, within a year, I was pregnant.

13

Baby, Baby, Baby

*'I was loving being a mum and I couldn't imagine trying
to juggle the old and new parts of my life.'*

My second birth story is the best of the three and should ideally
be shared around a kitchen table with a large glass of wine. It's
one of the top anecdotes of my life and I will admit to having
told the tale many times before. But before we get to that, I will
start at the beginning with Ernie and the moment I became
a mum.

I wafted through my first pregnancy in 2015 at the age of
thirty-two, certain in the knowledge that once I had our baby,
nothing was going to change. I had grand plans of going back
to work and a vision for how the baby would fit easily into our

busy lives. How hard could it be, I reasoned? I didn't realise that everything was going to change – and so it should. I know I am not the only expectant mother to have been in denial. I stopped working when I was seven months pregnant and it was the first time in my adult life that I had spent any length of time at home. Richie was playing for Warrington so we had moved to a lovely little house which backed on to a canal in Stockton Heath. It was idyllic. I was in full nesting mode for a couple of months: sorting out cupboards, organising paperwork and decorating the nursery.

My patience wore thin once the baby was a week overdue. I tried everything to hurry him up, including lots of acupuncture, and I danced around the house like mad the night before I went into labour. The following day my contractions started and I arrived at Whiston Hospital with the intention of having a water birth. This hope disappeared when the baby's heart rate began dropping so they needed to keep monitoring him. Just before he was born, when the pain was excruciating, I begged the midwife for drugs, but I had left it too late. She said, 'Of all the people who need the painkillers, you don't! You can handle it!' And through gritted teeth, I said, 'I've got nothing to prove!' She had that look that I had seen on the faces of the camera crew when they knew I was considering dropping out of the eighty-mile race. And so I pushed on. Literally.

It was quite dramatic because the cord was around the baby's neck, so the obstetrician wanted to use a ventouse (suction cup). I begged for one last chance to try to push him out on my own and amazingly, it worked. Out popped Ernie and my heart burst with love. OK, so it had not been the tranquil experience I had been imagining for the last few months. My birth plan had gone completely awry, which is funny when I think about it now, because how many women get to have the labour they want?! Particularly the first time around. I mentioned my disappointment to my friend Kim soon after and she said, 'What are you talking about? Nobody ever says "Congratulations! You were born in water!" What matters is that he was born safely.' She has always had an uncanny ability to stop me before I wind myself into a whirlwind. Hang onto those friends. We all need them.

From the moment Ernie was born, he was never a sleeper. It was June so the weather was lovely and I would take him out in his pram with our old dog, Barney, always trotting alongside. It was precious and I loved being out and about with him. At home, his nursery was kitted out with all the stuff you are told you should have but don't really need. I was in a glorious newborn bubble, thrilled with our little family of three.

Within a few months, we found out that Richie's contract for Warrington was not going to be renewed and he had an offer from a French team, Catalans Dragons in Perpignan in the South of France. We had moved from Wilmslow to Warrington and I was settled, so it was stressful to think about upping sticks and moving again, this time to a different country. Sport careers are similar to telly jobs in that you never quite know what is next and where you will be so you need to be open to change, but it was particularly hard because we now had Ernie. I was upset to leave behind our families, friends, the home we had created and the dreams I'd had for Ernie's first few years. I felt guilty about taking our baby away from our parents – my parents were born to be grandparents, they're better than the best – but I figured it was only for a couple of years and they could come out and see us for a holiday. We moved to France in October 2015 and it turned out to be the right decision.

I willingly put my career on hold. It's a brave step to take in my industry, where you can be forgotten in an instant, but I had a new baby so the timing was ideal. We rented a penthouse apartment overlooking the Mediterranean and I took Ernie to the beach every day. It was blissful, particularly in the summer. He never slept, so I would walk up and down the promenade with him, clocking hundreds of kilometres. I was telling Ernie about it recently and saying how often we would be up together at 5am watching the sunrise. I didn't want Richie being tired at training, so I used to lie in the living room with Ernie on blankets and cushions and watch the sun come up. A baby keeping you up all night is tough going but you can hardly complain when you're watching the sun rise over the Mediterranean with a day of no commitments or obligations stretching ahead of you.

Being in France gifted me the chance to be a full-time mum and have my baby all to myself without the work pressures and interruptions of being back in the UK. Richie would come back after training each day and the three of us would go out for dinner together, Ernie sleeping in his pram next to us while we ate. It was a stripped back, simplistic, wholesome life and, from my point of view, it was bliss. I shopped at markets, rarely had to battle the car seat drama, didn't have any other mums judging me or comparing notes as I didn't know anyone, and more often than not, my baby and I had sand between our toes.

From a rugby perspective, it was an extreme environment to go into. Rugby League is quite small in the UK and mainly happens along the M62, in places like Wigan, Warrington and Leeds, while in Australia it is like the Premier League and everything is big: clubs, player profiles, money. Some of the biggest names in the Australasian NRL ended up in France following stints of bad behaviour at the same time we were there. I have so much affection for and many great memories of that club, but it was hardcore. There were times when I would bump into the frazzled coach in the supermarket and he would say he was really happy on a Monday morning if none of his players had ended up in jail or hospital over the weekend. Recently, one of the old players who is now a coach compared our time there to the film *The Hangover*. It was often carnage and I know how hard the club has worked to turn the page on that chapter.

It may have been event-filled in the background but I was naïvely entertained by some of the antics and have always had a soft spot for the loveable, charming, idiot type of guy, and there were a few around. I was flattered that the single players wanted to come to our house at Christmas as we had a tree and a turkey. I was amused by their tales and thought those days were behind us. I have nothing but fond and happy memories of my time there.

For the first year, we were the only English family there, other than the player Jodie Broughton, but he was at a different stage of life. The French families were very kind to us but they had their own lives. It was lonely at times, but not in a bad way. I was free of the expectations that come with being a new mum because I was in a foreign country where nobody knew me. I didn't have to worry about unannounced guests, competitive NCT groups and trying to get out of my pyjamas. My life was like being on one long holiday and I had freedom and anonymity.

In the second year, the club had a clear-out of the mischief makers and brought in new guys with families who became firm friends. I was very much my own person, but being the wife of a full-time sportsman is inevitably all-consuming as their schedule dictates where you live and when you can holiday and socialise. You have to navigate injuries and operations as well as contracts being renewed or torn up. Sport is irrational in many wonderful ways – you win and emotions are high; you lose or get injured and there's an atmosphere that can consume a household. I enjoyed it but it's no easy ride, although it was made easier by the amazing lifestyle and opportunities presented by the club in France.

We moved to a villa with a pool, a five-minute walk from the beach and an hour from the mountains, and friends came over all the time. It was a dream life. If I thought about going back to work, it felt stressful. I was loving being a mum and I couldn't imagine trying to juggle the old and new parts of my life. Pre-baby, I felt obliged to take on a lot of telly work, worried I would offend people by saying no to things, but living in France meant I had an excuse to be selective. I did a couple of big but quick jobs while we were living there, but that was it.

I covered the 2016 European Swimming World Championships and the swimming and diving in the Olympics in Rio for BBC Sport because it was a short, defined amount of time away from home rather than having to disappear every couple of weeks. The Olympics were huge for me. After it, I got a lot of opportunities – which, again, I gladly turned down. People always have me down as some sort of career-obsessed working mum, but I have as much admiration for women who choose to give up their career as I do for those who juggle both or who choose not to have kids. I don't think there's a right way, there's your way and that's fine. Was it easier in our mums' day, when women with kids weren't expected to work? Who knows. Has the opportunity to work given us equality and a side serving of guilt? This is a Prosecco-fuelled debate my friends and I often have.

Not long after Rio, I found out I was pregnant again, and I had Louis in our second season of living in France. By now, I had friends, and I had bought a paddleboard (before they were even a thing) because never again did I think I would live next to the Mediterranean Sea. Another unusual thing about being married to a sportsperson is the need to get on with your partner's team mates and their other halves. I don't know if it happens in any other job, but I guess we all shared a life experience that saw us in random cities around the world through no fault of our own. There were partners who I immediately clicked with and will stay bonded to for life, and none more so than Jill Moa. Richie, Louis and I will forever be in her debt.

Picture the scene. It was April 2017 and we were happily settled in France. Ernie was not yet two years old and I was pregnant again. The French maternity system was quite different to what I was used to and much more blunt than I expected. For example, one doctor talked to me about breastfeeding, saying, 'If you breastfeed then great for the baby, if you don't then better for your boobs.' I was also recommended a Pilates course run by midwives because it would be 'good for your husband after you have had the baby'. I was amused to hear such a thing!

Richie was flying back to the UK every other week to play matches, but that was OK because I wasn't due for a few weeks. While the team was away, the wives would come over to our villa with their children and we would spend the day around the pool. After one of these lovely socials, I went to bed knowing I had overdone it. The next day, I went into labour. I was in the house with a twenty-month-old and my husband was in a different country. At first, I tried to pretend I wasn't in labour. I called Richie to say I was having twinges but thought it may be a false alarm. I think he could tell something was wrong from my voice so he called our friend Jill, who lived nearby, and told her he thought I was in labour but was trying to play it down. In the meantime, I had messaged the friendship WhatsApp group to say I was feeling rough so would anyone be able to take Ernie for a couple of hours? Ernie had never been anywhere other than by my side or with my mum, Richie or his mum at this point, so to even ask that was massive for me.

Within what felt like seconds, I knew the baby was on its way and I needed to get to the hospital. It's amazing what your brain does in these unprecedented situations, particularly when you are in a foreign country and aren't sure of the protocol. *I know what I will do*, I thought, *I will find my car keys and drive to the hospital once Ernie has been picked up*. Delirious, clearly. I got almost as far as the front door and couldn't stand up. I was on my hands and knees, roaring like a woman who is about to give birth, and Ernie, thinking we were playing dinosaurs, began hitting me over the head with a plastic sword. Then all hell broke loose.

First, one of my friends, Erin, who had seen my WhatsApp, arrived to collect Ernie. She took one look at me and went very pale. She had had a C-section with her baby and had no idea how to help, so she got Ernie an ice cream out of the freezer to keep him occupied. Then Jill turned up just in time and delivered the baby. She literally caught him as she walked through the door. We have never talked through the detail of exactly what happened but I think it's fair to say she was in the deep end in every sense of the word. We had bonded before over our views on motherhood, work and life in general, and she has a wicked sense of humour. I miss that now that we don't live within five minutes and a croissant from each other. To say I tested our friendship that day is putting it politely. If you know, you know. She held my Louis before I could. I just hadn't expected him to come so soon or in such a dramatic fashion. I was besotted with my Ernie and still unsure if I could love a second child as much as a first (you can, by the way), and then here he was, in the kitchen. I couldn't have wished for a more wonderful woman to hold him for a few moments while I got myself together and I hope her magic rubbed off on him in his first minutes in this world. If so, he will be more than fine.

However, I am afraid that this wasn't even the HALF OF IT. Someone had called for an ambulance but the way it works in France is that the message goes out to the nearest emergency service. It was just my luck it would be a fire engine. There I was, stark naked, clutching a tiny baby, watched over by two friends in shock, with a rampaging toddler and no husband or family closer than a plane journey away. In strode Vincent and Romain, in full fireman uniform. They both became emotional at the birth scene in front of them. They gushed about how they chose to be firemen to help people, but often this meant them visiting terrible scenes so they were overjoyed to walk into a happy one. 'Guys,' I said. 'That's lovely but can we talk later? Because I really need to get to hospital.' Before I left, I FaceTimed Richie from the kitchen and he asked who the guys were in the background. 'The firemen and your new son!' I said. He was emotional, frantic and desperately trying to get back to France. He was en route but still two flights away, as his best bet was to fly back via Barcelona.

I arrived at the hospital in the back of a fire truck, covered in a blanket, sitting next to an angle grinder, with nothing but a baby boy. There then ensued a terrible faff because, unlike with the NHS, I had to pay for healthcare upfront before receiving reimbursement, so they needed a credit card. A further complication was that the law states the baby needs to be registered there and then, which requires paperwork including a marriage certificate. These things were in storage. It was also expected that I stay in hospital for five days. I had nothing on me and I was distracted by the idea that Ernie was at home with Erin. It was very stressful. Everyone was speaking at once and I couldn't keep up. 'Please speak slowly,' I kept saying. 'French isn't my first language.'

The baby was whisked off to be checked because he weighed in at a small 5lbs 6oz, and I was put on a hospital bed with my feet in stirrups. Vincent and Romain, bless their hearts, were still there, standing at the end of the bed, talking to me from between my knees. 'Boys!' I said. 'Can you please come up near my head? It feels like I have just pushed a human through my nostril and I don't want you talking to me from down there!' The nurses were quite brutal, manhandling me and not explaining what they were doing. I had just given birth, I had two emotional firemen looking at my bits, no paperwork, a husband in a different country, another child at home, my new baby had been whisked away and I couldn't understand what was going on. It was surreal.

Mum managed to get a flight over that day, so she went straight to the house, picked up Ernie and they came to visit me. Ernie met his baby brother and was pretty nonplussed, seeming completely unaffected by the drama. Richie got back that night and stayed for twenty-four hours before he had to return to the UK for a match as there was no paternity leave.

After two Rugby League seasons, we returned to the UK in 2018. I wasn't ready to come back; I wanted to stay out there longer. I was happy with my new identity of not working much, being a mum and wandering to the farmer's market to pick up dinner. Richie got offered an extension from Catalans and I desperately hoped he would accept it. We didn't really discuss it because at the same time Leeds offered him a contract, sent the paperwork and he signed it. I can remember watching him as he talked to the Leeds manager, our bright blue swimming pool between us, a vineyard filling the view behind him, as the sun was setting. It's poetic I guess, but I honestly remember that moment as clearly as if it was yesterday, which is unusual given that I often forget where I've parked my car at the supermarket. I can still see everything in my mind's eye in that moment he agreed the deal that would see us leave France.

He and I may recall this differently. I know he thought it would be good for us to be closer to our families now we had two children. He knew that at some point I would miss work and it would be impossible to travel as easily as I had with just one baby. Also, Leeds was a bigger club and he could see a life after rugby there. All valid points, but something had changed at the Catalan club too. There had been a falling-out and Richie was now on the periphery of the team.

The next thing I knew, we were packing up to move home and I wasn't alright about it. It took me a long time to accept it. It was probably selfish of me because I wasn't ready to be back in the UK or to have to think about work again. I loved my career but I had really enjoyed taking a break from it. Supporting my husband in the South of France had been the perfect excuse for a long maternity leave. I remember it so fondly and have stayed in touch with the French wives, who have been good friends to me.

Now we come to the last baby, the one who transformed our family from four to five. In 2021, I was pregnant again. This time around, I was classed as high risk because of Louis' premature arrival and my age – considered an old mum at thirty-eight. We were living in Leeds by now. Friends thought we were mad to have another baby as the boys were out of nappies and Ernie was about to go to school. Why go back to the beginning? Why indeed. It wasn't about trying for a girl. Richie and I talked about it for a long time. We were in a really nice position because we had just moved into a house we had spent a couple of years working on. We had pored over every inch together: the sockets, the sinks, the fireplaces. Each one had a story we shared and it was exactly how we wanted it. We had our dream home with our dream garden, two gorgeous boys and we were in a good place in our relationship. It wasn't something we entered into lightly; we always used to joke about how having two children meant we could 'man mark' them and we knew that once we had a third we would be outnumbered, but we were up for it. It just felt right to try for one more baby. Was I hoping for a girl? Genuinely, no. Am I glad I have one? Hell, yes.

The doctors at Leeds Maternity Hospital thought the baby was going to be small and I would probably need a C-section. The staff were fantastic and they kept a close eye on me towards the end of the pregnancy. I was in and out of hospital so they could monitor me but, even though I had the boys to look after and work commitments, I was fine. On Christmas Eve, I thought I was going into labour so I went straight to hospital, only to discover it was a false alarm, which was a relief because I wanted to be at home when the boys woke up and opened their presents. I did not feel at all well on Christmas Day and a positive Covid test coincided with the early stages of labour. At that time, medical opinion was that catching Covid in late pregnancy could be dangerous, so I was swiftly admitted back into hospital. There were strict visiting rules which meant my parents had the boys and Richie brought me in food and said he was my 'lido' – by which he really meant doula but he couldn't remember the word! My labour was progressing slowly and the midwife said she was off for a break so, if things hadn't moved along sufficiently by the time she was back, she would induce me. Within an hour, I went from being 3cm to 9cm dilated. I gave birth to our bouncing baby girl naturally in the early hours of 28 December, and Richie and I, exhausted and elated, took her home a few hours later. By midday, the five of us were on the sofa. Elsie was here and our family was complete.

14

Rio Olympics

*'It was all going so well – and then there was
a post on Twitter about my legs.'*

While I was in France, I was asked to present the BBC's
swimming coverage for the Rio Olympics in 2016. It meant
a couple of weeks away from home but it was a fantastic
opportunity so I jumped at the chance. The options for shopping for outfits in the South of France were either markets
or designer stores, so I employed a fab stylist, Cobbie Yates,
who has an incredible dedication to his craft. I didn't think
too hard about what I was wearing; I have never been that
sort of TV presenter. I always love it if someone else can dress
me and I trusted Cobbie's professional eye; he worked hard to

find independent brands and great designers that he knew I would enjoy wearing.

Being in Rio was incredible. I am sure I overuse that word but in this instance it's definitely the right one to describe the experience. There is no better job for someone who has been brought up around sport. I was in the middle of history being made with an 'access all areas' pass so I went to everything: the football final, the 100m final, the gymnastics. I saw Matt Whitlock win medals. The Olympic pool was full of drama, with our team including Tom Daley, Adam Peaty and Fran Halsall, who missed out by a fingernail. I was reporting alongside legendary swimmers Rebecca Adlington and Mark Foster. They were so well connected that guests were falling over themselves to come into the studio to be interviewed. We were able to freestyle a lot of the time because we didn't have a heavy production schedule. In addition, the GB swim team were winning loads of medals. Unlike in some other sports where very little was happening, we were right in the thick of it. It was all going so well – and then there was a post on Twitter about my legs.

I was wearing shorts. Cobbie had sent clothes that were comfortable in a hot climate but also smart enough for the screen. We sat at a table on high bar stools and I assumed the shots would be from the table up. Some of the time we didn't even have shoes on. It was Rio, it was hot for goodness' sake! As

Boxing for Sports Relief. I loved the boxing training; it was the fittest I have ever been. Coached by a man I will forever be in awe of, Phil Sellars.

SAS Who Dares Wins … brutal but brilliant, I would go back into it in a heartbeat. In the back of a truck with fellow contestants Joey Essex and Locksmith, probably having just been dropped out of a helicopter backward into a lake.

Travels with my tribe, en route back from France via Bordeaux and beyond.

My first baby with my second real baby. Louis and Barney the *Blue Peter* dog who joined and left the show with me.

Covering the World Swimming Championships in 2017 in Budapest for the BBC. Mum travelled with me, making it possible.

At Wentworth playing in the Pro Am alongside Dan Walker and Andy Sullivan, whilst I was six months pregnant with Elsie.

Taking a swing! Golf is something I love now and will continue to play with my family.

Covering the rugby for Channel 4. I always enjoy being out on the field, witnessing the action and commentating alongside it.

Strictly Come Dancing. The talent of
the hair and makeup on that team
know no bounds.

Tyler and Molly brought the vibes and
energy, Hamza brought the biceps
to hoist me up.

Waltzing into the final (sorry!).

Gorka Marquez. The man who got me on the dance floor, humoured my inability to remember the steps and bought me A LOT of cinnamon buns.

The class of 2022.
Good people.
Good times.
Grateful for each
and every one.

With Fleur in glad rags and Elly in comfies. I have so much love and respect
for these women, sharing laughs, secrets, and pizza.

On the *Strictly* tour doing the number from cabaret, Anton said
it elicited the kind of reaction performers live for. Will I ever experience
a crowd roar like that again? Forever thankful.

Mucking about with my partner Kai on tour, the man with the quite possibly the biggest smile in telly. Very appreciative that he stepped in to do the tour alongside me.

With Dad in Blackpool. Having the children, my family and my friends at the tower ballroom was what it was all about for me.

Dining out with mum and dad. My team.

On the Pennines filming adventures with Dan Walker.

Feel so much joy in water,
with our labrador, Spider-Man.
No prizes for guessing who
named him.

This is forty.
Entering my fifth decade,
entertained by the children,
with good friends and feeling
grateful to be doing a job I love:
live telly and radio.

the show finished, a couple of people said there had been a few mentions on social media, but I was a bit oblivious to it until my brother rang and asked me why Dad was on *This Morning*. Ruth Langsford and Eamonn Holmes were interviewing him about whether women (me) were being victimised for wearing shorts and he said, 'I thought we were past talking about what women wear. We should be talking about what women do. I think Matt, Becky and Helen are doing a great job, and isn't this a bit disrespectful to the swimmers who have trained for years to take part in this competition?' I was so proud of him! Ruth was in full support. The media interest exploded and journalists even turned up at my parents' house, where Mum made them all a cuppa, 'because they have travelled a long way, Helen'.

As much as I wish we lived in a different society now, we know what sells newspapers and in this instance it wasn't Mark Foster looking dashing in a nice shirt. It was some blonde bird with her legs out. Look, I am not complaining but it was not my intention to be the topic of conversation for anything other than my job, presenting the Olympic swimming. I wasn't trying to upstage anyone; Cobbie was helping me to feel good in my first post-baby job, and that in turn made me feel more professionally confident. I genuinely didn't think you could even see my legs as we were sitting at a desk, so I assumed they were hidden under it. The irony is that, in my family, we women are known for having big legs. To this day, my cousin Kerry will not permit a full-length picture for social media due to the family leg curse. I don't care. I know I have a big set of legs and I've had plenty of comments on social media about my 'pie legs', but they have served me well. What it does mean, though, is that IF I was going to intentionally flash a part of my body, it would not be my legs. Kerry would simply not allow it.

The media interest was out of control and it was one of the many times in my career when I have just bitten my tongue and said nothing while people say something about me. It's a part of the job that I have had to learn to be OK with. I had the same issue when I got *Blue Peter* and there was a double-page spread with a headline referring to me as a 'champagne swilling WAG'. This was all because my boyfriend at the time played football and there was a picture on my Facebook page of me at a wedding with a drink. Joel was put out that there was no mention of him as the new boy and I told him to be careful what he wished for. We've talked many times since about how glad he is that he didn't get splashed over the front pages back when we started. It happened a few times and I got more attention than the boys. I wasn't sure it was a good thing. Of course, it's hard to say because I may not have had the career I've had without it. It doesn't mean it's easy, though, to have no control over what is said and the conclusions people will draw from that. It comes with the job so I know I can't complain about the media because I chose to be in the public eye.

As for me and the shorts, I just wanted to be cool and comfortable. There was a lull in medal-winning, which gave an opportunity for the analysis to continue, with discussions about whether I should have used a stylist, was I a victim of misogyny and did anyone remember why we were actually there?! Sharron Davies was lovely to me. She had been through the same and she told me not to take it personally. She was right.

When I talk about Rio, I hate that I even mention the shorts because all that should be said about Rio should be about our athletes. Adam Peaty was amazing, Fran Halsall came so close, Jack Laugher and Chris Mears made history and Tom Daley displayed some of the most human qualities on the biggest stage ever. It was a professional chapter I am so thankful for because we were able to showcase amazing young people doing amazing things. Talking to Tom Daley after he lost in his bid to win gold after starting so strongly was one of the best and worst interviews I'veever had to do. He didn't want to be on telly in that moment. I had watched him ringside since he was a boy; I wanted to hug him and pack him off to his mum, but instead I had to put a microphone under his nose. God bless his grace – and I confess, the tiny hack in me was glad I was the one who got to hold that microphone, but it wasn't pleasant.

At Rio, we were ringside as a generation of athletes made the world realise Great Britain is really good at swimming and diving, and it inspired the next generation to go for it. To say we had fun presenting is putting it mildly – we laughed all day, every day, on and off screen. We wanted the nation to experience the atmosphere and joy that we were, and we wanted the athletes to know how much their dedication was appreciated. I hope we did that. I have been in the public eye to a lesser or greater extent for over eighteen years and so much of what is written about me doesn't bother me. If it did, I think I would have given up onthe industry by now and gone off to be a paddleboard instructor. Maybe I have got used to it, but I certainly don't google myself, even recently when my personal life was in the papers. I take no more notice of the good press than I do the bad press. The idea of my shorts being a symbol for women victimised in the media made me feel uncomfortable because nobody should be defined by how they look or what they wear, but they often are. I didn't wear them with any particularintent or thought. I just got up one morning and put on a pair of shorts.

Invitations to events and corporate jobs ramped up after 'shortsgate' at Rio, but I turned them down because I wanted to go home to my family. Back in France, my pregnancy with Louis was beginning to show and the stories suddenly changed from me in sexy shorts to how much weight I had piled on. I would like to say I was smart enough not to let it affect me, but it did. I was so happy to be back in France and hoped that the press interest would die down quickly. I wasn't sure

I wanted to play the game anymore. It was a relief to have escaped the microscopic attention and be anonymous again. I was back in leggings with my hair scraped into a ponytail, make-up free and wandering around the market looking for ripe peaches. It was so liberating. True JOMO.

Back in 2012, I presented the Olympic homecoming in London with Ben Shephard outside Buckingham Palace. All the Olympians were transported down the Mall in open-top buses and there was a carnival atmosphere. I was on stage about to interview David Cameron when a sudden gust of wind whipped up the skirt of my red dress in front of the thousands there. I was clueless. The parade was also being simulcast on every network. I don't even want to think how many people would have been watching. The whole crowd cheered and I thought, *Blimey, David Cameron is more popular than I realised.* He looked at me, pointed at my skirt and said, 'Well handled.' And I thought, *What on earth is he talking about?*

When we came off air, Ben Shephard took my phone and said, 'Let's go for a drink first, shall we?' He very cleverly, and kindly, made sure I had a gin before I was made aware of the situation. When I eventually got my phone back I had countless messages from people saying, 'You've just flashed your pants!' I wouldn't have minded so much if they were nice pants, but I had just come back from a filming trip so they weren't first- pick pants. I hadn't done my washing so they were my big apple-catchers! I remember someone tweeted saying, 'How irresponsible! She should have had haberdashery weights in her skirt hem.' Recently, my kids were watching a programme about things that shouldn't happen to TV presenters and I was on it flashing my knickers, forever embedded on the internet. They were genuinely thrilled.

15

Sporting Chance

*'I think the biggest lesson from my work in sport is legacy.
I got out of it what I put in.'*

In the summer, on a Friday evening, you will often find me at the local cricket club as my boys have started to play. The setting is idyllic and my friends' and relations' kids play too. The bar is cheap and the music is good, so throw in some warm weather and it's fair to say this feels like a parenting win. When the sun is shining, the boys are laughing and the baby is running around, then I know I made the right decision to move back to the Lakes. Of all the sidelines I stand on, this one is the most social. All thanks to the coaches for their patience and effort in running kids' sports clubs.

Sporting Chance

Occasionally, the cricket or football coach will mention how my boys are progressing and I say all I need to know is if they are polite and are good team members. For me, it's not about them being the best; it's about the enjoyment they get from it. If they choose to be competitive then great, but it is not for me to be that on their behalf. That said, I get really emotional when I watch them. I cried when Louis took part in a cross-country race recently and I sobbed when Ernie came second in a skipping race. Maybe I will grow out of it but I suspect not.

When I was younger, Mum often played sport with us, whether it was football, cricket, netball or tennis. I don't under-estimate how much that shaped me and my brother in our early years. I went on to play netball at the infamous Brough village hall, later the scenes of my teen nights out – what a venue! Everything happened there. I played hockey at school, but I wasn't very good at it, and I played badminton at a club my mum ran in our local village hall, which was very popular with the youth. Mum still hammers us now if we play. She doesn't believe in letting us win either. She is the same with her grandchildren. She was playing cricket with Ernie in the garden and he asked, 'Granny, were you good at sport at school?' She said she had been very good. He said, 'It's really hard to believe, isn't it Granny?' Out of the mouths of babes and all that.

Dad is mad into football and, from a young age, my brother, Gavin, would be kicking a ball around outside every night. He would be in full strip and I would put on a matching t-shirt and shorts to try and emulate his football kit. My family on both my mum and my dad's sides support Carlisle United and would go to every home game. Gavin was a very talented youth player and attended the Manchester United and Nottingham Forest academies. He began playing professionally for our beloved Carlisle United with players who went on to the Premier League, so he was one of an excellent generation of footballers. It's a difficult career to navigate and there were a lot of questions around whether he would make it or not. I think he has made it because he has forged an entire life around his passion. He has played in cup finals, European championships and is now assistant manager for Carlisle United. Is he a World Cup goal-scoring Premier League footballer? No. Has he made a job out of something he loves? Yes. That's a success in my eyes. My kids are crazy proud of him. And so am I.

Football was stitched into my childhood and, in returning home, I have rediscovered it a little. I can't profess to being a dedicated supporter but I get it; it's a sense of belonging, of being part of something. An identity for some, I guess. When I first moved to London, I found weekends hard, with no structure, family or friends, so I started watching Brentford. They played down the road from me and for a time I would go, sometimes alone, and I knew the kind of people who would be on the terraces. It felt familiar and a home away from home. In moving back to Cumbria, Carlisle offered the same. I can find any of my cousins, aunties or uncles on a Saturday afternoon at Brunton Park. Being there was a great way to ease me back ont o home turf and into single life. Lots of people have talked to me about how hard Sundays can be when you are newly single. My advice is to take up golf or adopt a local team. Bury yourself in something new and active.

Football offers something more tribal. I imagine it's a similar feeling people may get if they go to church or to a rave. Football is not just a community but a way for families to bond. I love that my kids and my nephews experience this with older generations of their family and they are united in the conversations around the matches. We all went to Wembley to watch Carlisle United beat Stockport County and secure their promotion to Sky Bet League One. It was an indescribable moment to see Gavin, his family and the team's hard work rewarded. My kids ran around swinging their tops over their heads, screaming until they were hoarse, jumping on the backs of strangers and hugging them as if they were family. The joy on my parents' faces was priceless and I was so thankful to Gavin after they had been by his side through years of the massive highs and lows the sport brings.

Now I have my own children I know how this feels, as I stand on the sideline and watch every tackle, every dropped ball, every missed opportunity. I live it with them. My children are tiny and it's for fun, but already I can see why parents stress, tempers flare and emotions spill over. Mum and Dad, I am sorry Gavin has taken you to your wits' end! Aren't you glad I wasn't that good at sport? Dad lives for football and his kids, so to see his son lift the trophy at Wembley was amazing. Gavin kindly brought the trophy into the boys' school a couple of weeks later, which they were absolutely thrilled about.

Without sport, I doubt my boys would have been able to slot into their new community as quickly and easily as they have. What helped Ernie adapt was an invitation from two of the boys in the village to join their football team, coupled with a warm welcome from the team's coach, Paul Cooper. Small acts of kindness that I will never take for granted. He joined the cricket team too. Louis is the only boy in his year so it's good for him to go to sport clubs and mix with other boys his age too. It's a great discipline and they will often go and train in the garden of their own accord. If I am working, Dad gets a lot of joy from taking them to their sport clubs, which makes my heart sing. It is also reminiscent of the old days, when he took Gavin everywhere to play football. One of the dads who helps at my son's football training told me he would never have played the game as a child if it wasn't for my dad because his parents wouldn't take him. Dad would give him lifts to training and matches when he was taking my brother and he says he is forever grateful to him. Now he is teaching my boys.

When I was a rugby wife, I tried to go to every game Richie played in and took the kids with me too. I really enjoyed supporting him from the sidelines and at the end of each match, I would go down to the pitch with the kids so we could capture the moment in a photo. We were embedded in the rugby club family and the boys even modelled the Leeds Rhino kit for a photoshoot. There was never any question that Richie's career took precedent because I understood how sport worked. Being married to a sportsman was exciting. I was proud of him, and of the clubs he played for, and the kids loved going training with him to see their daddy at work. I always joke with friends who are married to rugby players that rugby kids are different because they think nothing of running head-first into each other.

Rugby life gave me such a mad, eclectic, wonderful collection friends. Sport is transient, so you make a lot of acquaintances and some really good friends. Our group was a mix of Samoan, Tongan, Australian and northern English families who dropped into and out of our lives. One of the positives of that time of life is I was left with great friends who shared key moments, like our children taking their first steps together. I show the boys photographs of these times and we are planning to meet up with people this summer, with a big trip to Australia at some point in the future. We all had so much fun and our houses in France and Leeds were always full of rugby families who brought food, drink and a lot of laughter. One of my favourite memories is of a Tongan player, Koni, who said he would organise a barbecue at ours. I was expecting burgers and sausages, but he got scaffolding delivered, built a spit and roasted a pig. He apologised that he had to buy the pig because, back in Tonga, he would have just gone out and caught it. I still keep in touch with many of the friends I hung out with back then, or I will bump into people through my work with the rugby league and it's lovely to see them.

Sport is a huge part of my job too. From my early work with local radio and television, I have covered a huge number of different sports. When I joined BBC *Sportsround*, every Saturday I would be sent to Premier League grounds to where the *Match of the Day* cameras were stationed. I would film a preview of the game, which took a matter of minutes, and then I was free to stay and watch the match. As sports journalist jobs go, it was super easy, and as a football fan, it was ace!

I first started working for BBC Radio 5 Live when I was still on *Blue Peter* and I have continued to work for them on and off ever since. My first assignment was covering Wimbledon in 2010. I couldn't believe my jammy luck. I was going to be working alongside some of the most incredible commentators in the world and my role was to be out in the crowds and on Henman Hill to find personal interest soundbites.

I turned up to the production office on the first day and in my telly way, I threw my arms around everyone to hug them. Apparently, this was not done. They preferred to shake hands. I felt so uncomfortable and intimidated, but they were lovely to me. I was working with John Hunt, John Inverdale, Alistair Bruce-Ball, Russell Fuller, David Law and Clare Balding, and knew it didn't get any better than that. Sensing I was feeling like an amateur, Alistair said, 'Listen, Helen, you can't do what they do and they can't do what you do.' That has always stuck with me. I couldn't talk about Novak Djokovic's serve or win ratios, but they couldn't go on the hill and find a bloke who had spent his life savings flying over from Auckland and had slept outside for three days. That said, I did update on one of the most important matches of the tournament by complete accident. I was sent to cover John Isner's game against Nicolas Mahut on one of the smaller courts and it became the longest match in history, at eleven hours and five minutes, earning a world record in the process.

I was out of my depth at Wimbledon to begin with. The hours were very long. It was all new and, in the grown-up land of serious broadcasting, public and private critiques can be harsh. I had a lot of fun, though, and would ask if I could do crazy things to create great content, like, 'Can I have a barbecue on the roof?' No, you can't, Helen. I was full of energy and buzzing with annoying ideas! I would sit in the commentary box listening to Jonathan Overend, whose commentary was pure poetry. I was watching the world's best tennis players and listening to the world's best commentators at one of the world's best sporting venues. This was my job. I had to pinch myself.

When I left *Blue Peter*, the TV presenter Jake Humphrey recommended me to the team at BT Sport – a new channel with big ambitions and an even bigger budget. They were pushing boundaries and doing maverick things like putting in glass studio floors, so I figured taking a gamble on a chirpy and sociable kids' telly presenter wasn't too left field. I joined the daily news show as well as Tim Lovejoy's weekend programme, covering women's football and conference football. It was commercial telly so the atmosphere was more relaxed, a bit like a pub where everyone is a couple of drinks away from things getting a little out of hand!

We were sent on shopping trips to get the right clothes and the hair and make-up teams polished and preened us. The green room was always full of big names and the production team were up for trying anything. It was a very fun place to work. I could suggest crazy ideas and they would say, 'How much will it cost? Let's do it!' For one segment with an American basketball team, I was positioned by the hoop holding the ball, while a player ran forward, jumped on a trampoline, somersaulted, took the ball off me and slam dunked. In rehearsal, he completed it but landed on me, knocking me over. I thought it was hilarious and said we should cut the film into the programme like a blooper, but the cameraman was horrified. He said I was an inch away from paralysis and he didn't think we should show it, and the team agreed.

BT Sport was a brilliant employer and they helped me transition from leaving the flagship success of *Blue Peter*. It prevented me from pining too long and hard for the last five years of my life. I also met the fantastic producer Stephen Cook, who has remained a colleague and friend ever since. Years later, he suggested me for the Rugby League reporting for Channel 4. I wasn't sure because it was Richie's area and I didn't want to blur the lines, but both Richie and Stephen persuaded me to do it in early 2022, and I still work on it today.

In my next sporting role, I was back at the BBC, covering the swimming and diving, treading in the epic footsteps of the brilliant Clare Balding and Gabby Logan. Clare was incredibly supportive and paved the way for me when she went off to do the main Olympics highlights show, and Gabby is one of the nicest women in the industry. I may not see her from one year to the next, but she and her husband Kenny are the sort of people I could call and ask to hide in their spare room for a week. I had a great few years covering the European and World Championships, the Olympics and the Commonwealth Games, following inspiring young athletes and their dedicated families. I arrived at a time when the British athletes were doing really well in swimming, so it was a gift of a job for a presenter to be interviewing winners. I was surrounded by a great group of people including Becky Adlington, Mark Foster and the awesome producer Michael Jackson. In addition, we had Sharron Davies poolside, with Adrian Moorhouse and Andy Jameson commentating. It was a dream team of talent and we all got on as mates. It's hard to replicate or fake the sort of energy we created between us. Working on the World Championships called for long days and we were exhausted. One day, Michael called a meeting and we trudged to it only to find he had hired us all bikes and booked an escape room. He believed in working hard and playing hard. Some TV producers have a natural gift for the role and he did.

Throughout this time, I dipped in and out of BBC Radio 5 Live, covering things like the horseracing at Epsom and Cheltenham. My job was to get the colour from the crowd. When I was doing those gigs I often worked with Chessie Bent, one of the absolute best sport producers, universally loved by all. Most recently, she produced my Sunday morning Radio 5 Live show. Chessie has always been very good at keeping me in check, so when I went off on a tangent at Wimbledon – maybe with a bloke from Brazil in a tent, while his wife cooked us chorizo on a camping stove – she would rein me back in. When it got too off-piste she would say in my ear, 'Back to John in the studio'. Even now, if I go off topic, she will say, 'Back to John'. It's become our catchphrase. The John we are referring to is John Inverdale. I am so fond of him. He was another champion of mine and was always very generous about including me in the programme as much as possible. He was so proud of his daughters, who were big hockey players, and he is a big supporter of women in sport.

Women's sport has changed so much during my career. I am pleased we have stopped comparing it to men's sport because it is different and I think this is more likely to drive participation. Women's football is its own thing. Let's focus on the game. I also respect the evolution of sports people using their platforms to raise awareness. Look at Marcus Rashford and his revolutionary school dinners campaign, or the England women's football team going out to play a game with only one in three players having their names on their shirts to raise awareness around dementia in partnership with the Alzheimer's Society. As a parent of sporty kids, I really appreciate the powerful message that this gives, demonstrating how the industry can do good on and off the field.

At my kids' football academy, more girls than boys turned up for the trials. Elsie has been walking since she was ten months old and I watch her kicking a ball in the garden while the pram and doll are discarded. She may come back to them but all she ever sees is her brothers playing football, and so at the moment, that's what she wants to do too. Nature or nurture, who knows? All of them will be whoever and what-ever they want to be, but I am grateful for the girls who have gone before them. My boys don't know any different – they see women's games on telly, they see girls at training and on their school team. As it should be.

When I started working in sport, there weren't as many female broadcasters as there are now. I didn't go in driven by a burning desire to change the agenda, I just liked sport and I understood it, having grown up with a brother whose life was dictated by football. I remember my first shift at *Newsround* meant I had to go and cover Fabio Capello's first game at Wembley, but I was mostly stressed about navigating the tube, not talking about football. I hadn't really considered the implications of being a female in a male-dominated world. I was friendly and smiley so people were nice to me. Did they think I was rubbish or an airhead? I don't know and I didn't really care.

I think this job carries a lot of responsibility and I am not afraid to point out to people if their language or their views could cause offence. I remember talking to one of the older football commentators, in his seventies, and he called a female player 'a fit bird'. I tapped him on the arm and said, 'Mate, just so you know, talking like that is really disrespectful; it will upset a lot of people and could probably get you fired.' And he said, 'Oh God, is that bad? I thought that was a compliment.' For some, it's like learning a new language. It's imperative they do.

In an interview a few years ago, I was asked about the #MeToo movement and whether I had ever been the victim of sexual harassment in the workplace. No, I said. They couldn't quite believe me. This may sound unbelievable, considering I work in the media and in sport, but it's true. I said that in my experience, sporting bodies are very supportive and protective. To demonstrate my point, I mentioned a brief situation that occurred when I was presenting from the World Darts Championship.

The darts is an interesting environment to navigate because of the high alcohol consumption. A lot of people there have one too many – absolutely no judgement, and in many ways it makes for a great atmosphere. One of the darts players came over to me to be interviewed on live television and he tapped me on the arse. I was pregnant with Ernie and caught off guard, so I let out a little squeal before regaining my professional composure. I was annoyed but didn't let it show. Behind the scenes, everything kicked off. The darts body got involved and the player in question was reprimanded. It was taken out of my hands before I even knew what was happening. I didn't have to consider whether to make a complaint or not; they dealt with it immediately.

I told this story, as I do again now, to describe how quickly and efficiently the incident was handled by the relevant authorities. The player was remorseful and that, I thought, was that. I didn't say who the player was or go into any detail. I didn't think it was a big deal. When the interview came out, the wider press picked up on this story and ran with it. Unfortunately, they misquoted the original piece and said I had been groped, which wasn't true. Then the darts player in question reacted to the stories and defended himself against the allegations, which I can understand as they were much exaggerated. The downside was that this fuelled the story and he outed himself in the process. So now everyone knew it was him and we were both exposed in a way neither of us wanted.

The public response was mostly anger towards me. There were those who said I should have spoken up and used my platform to support others dealing with sexual harassment and misogyny. Then there were others who asked why nobody can take a joke these days and said I was overreacting. It felt like a no-win situation. I was trying to shine a positive light on my experience, but once you open that Pandora's box you cannot control how the story unravels.

My point has always been that at every event I have worked at, whether as a single woman, heavily pregnant or breast-feeding, I have never felt disrespected or uncomfortable. And on the one occasion this was different, it was dealt with properly. It made me wish I had never said anything. I didn't think, *He shouldn't have done that to me and made me feel awkward.* I thought, *I shouldn't have mentioned it to a journalist.* I can see how people who have suffered far, far worse, do not feel able to speak up. Things get taken out of context and you have no control over the narrative. Should he have tapped me on the bottom? No, he should not, he absolutely shouldn't. But was he trying to be cheeky and engage in banter? Yes, he probably was. It went completely wrong.

Richie had a similar situation when he was playing rugby. There was an aggressive tackle and the bloke's finger went in his backside, which is an illegal thing to do. The other player claimed it was an accident but it was caught on camera. Richie was not going to take it further, but the situation was out of his hands and there was a subsequent investigation involving analysis and cross-referencing with doctors, physios and other members of the teams. The debate was whether it was accidental or intentional. It was difficult; Richie had not raised the complaint but as it was being dealt with he wanted to be honest and say he believed it was intentional. The other player received an eight-game ban for abusive behaviour, so he then went on to social media to put his side of the story across, which ignited the drama further.

As for misogyny, well, I have experienced my fair share of that. Here is an anecdote that sums it up. I was in the studio with a male presenter and the programme was running a thought-provoking video I had filmed. It cut back to us and the presenter said, 'I wouldn't have expected that from you.' Confused by what he meant, I said, 'Why?' He replied, 'Well, you can get away with most stuff because you're pretty but I wouldn't have expected something like that.' I think he meant I had done a good job. Somewhere in there was a compliment, but I had to dig really deep for it. One of my often-used phrases is, 'Right intention, wrong execution.'

Dad played golf and wanted me to give it a go, but I never had time. When Louis started school, I was approached by Kenny Logan to sign up for a celebrity golf academy, aimed at encouraging more women to take up the sport. I was offered six months of free golf lessons, golf clubs and as much gin as I could drink, alongside Fleur East, Bela Shah and Natalie Pinkham. We would then compete against each other to win a place in a Pro-Am golf tournament, which is where both professional and amateur golfers compete against one another. What's not to like?! I jumped at the chance.

I clicked instantly with my golf coach, Steph, and as soon as I started playing I was hooked on the game. My eye on the prize, I wanted not only to win, I wanted to be genuinely good. Or at least, good enough to get around a golf course without making a fool of myself. I loved playing with my dad and Richie – it was something we could do together and they were both very encouraging. Perhaps my biggest emotional win came from my boys because it was something they loved watching me do and wanted to be with me. They loved the driving range, seeing how far and fast the ball went as it was recorded on the driving range computers. They loved the 'WHACK' of the driver, and there were lots of proud shouts of 'Good one, Mum!' Thank God my coach was great with kids. Steph has her own children and was happy to have mine around (I think).

On the first day of training, in cold, wet January, we took a walk around the course so I could get my bearings and Ernie came too. Only my child could fall in a stream! Soaked from head to toe, we had to dash back to the car for a full change of clothes. Steph even pretended not to see when Louis did a wild wee on the second hole. It encouraged them to start playing too. Louis particularly loves it and regularly asks me or my dad to take him to the range. Judy Murray once said to me that when you have kids, you need to find a sport you can do with them as you all get older, and I think golf could be that for us. I would love to think that we will still be playing together as a family through their teenage years and beyond.

Golf lessons were a great distraction as both boys were at school. Not only did I love playing, I really enjoyed walking around the course and talking to people. No surprise for someone like me who loves to chat. We were based near the gin company which was sponsoring the academy and they would put on events where women could come and have a go in a friendly and inclusive atmosphere. I met a lot of amazing women of a certain age who had either returned to golf or were taking it up as their children were older and they had more time on their hands. They were too old to start sprint training but not willing to give up on sport, and they wanted to do something cool, so golf fitted their criteria. I took so much from the sessions and learned a huge amount from these women who were ahead of me on the parenting ladder. It brought me into contact with people I may not have met in my everyday life – it was a different demographic from football, rugby or boxing. My dad has played golf for years and he is nearly seventy, but because of the handicap system I can go out and have a decent match with him. It's not like running a marathon with someone who has never run one before. Golf is very levelling.

While I was training for the golf, I was also filming Channel 4's *Inside the Superbrands*, which involved a certain amount of travelling. Since I had children, I don't do overnights as a rule, unless there is no other option, but whenever I had to stay away, I took golf clubs with me so if I couldn't get home I would use that time to go to a driving range.

I wasn't very good, so I practised, played a lot and felt mildly confident by the time I got to the play-off at Wentworth. The stage was set; we had built up to this for months. The audience, lady captain and my competitors were all watching. Silence fell as, one after the other, Fleur, Natalie and Bela smashed their balls down the fairway. Then it was my turn. I miss-hit it and it went sideways into a bush. The stunned crowd paused, then clapped awkwardly. What followed was the worst seven holes I have ever played. Both Kenny Logan and my coach Steph said, 'You're not shit, so why are you playing shit?' And it really jolted me back into the game. I knew I was better than that. Dad was with me as a support too. Then I played the next seven holes really well and the eighteenth was almost the best hole I had played in my life, and I won. Which was a mixed blessing because then I had to play against professionals.

The Pro-Am tournament was also at Wentworth a few weeks later with an intimidating audience. I played in a team with TV pal Dan Walker and professional golfer Andy Sullivan, and they immediately put me at ease. Apparently, my inexperience and handicap was really useful to them, which meant I could contribute something to the team. Who knew?! Whoever drives it the furthest is where you play from, so Andy did that and then I putted it. I went into it thinking they would be mortified because I was the worst golfer there and instead they were thrilled because it played to our advantage. It automatically took the pressure off me and meant I could play without fear. I felt like a valid part of the team and loved the banter throughout.

I played that competition six months pregnant and at times I was rubbish, but until the final hole, we were winning! On the fourteenth, when the crowd was watching, I got a birdie, my best hole of the round in front of a stand full of people, with my Slingsby academy pals, Fleur and Nat, whooping from the tee. That hole and that feeling is enough to keep me going to the driving range with one eye on getting back to it properly one day when I have time.

After I had Elsie and Richie left, I found solace at the driving range. I would pop Elsie in the car and by the time I got there she would be asleep. I could carefully carry her out so as not to disturb her and take her up to the top bay on the roof. Steph booked it for me and I had an opportunity to knock out fifty balls before Elsie woke up. It also meant fresh air, exercise and escape. I am not an aggressive person but it gave me the same physical buzz I got from boxing. As much as I enjoyed punching a bag, so I loved whacking a little ball with a big stick. The sound and the feeling when you hit the sweet spot and it goes where you want it to go is heaven. It's so therapeutic.

I think the biggest lesson from my work in sport is legacy. I got out of it what I put in and I have continued to gain employment and work within a network made up of talented and loyal people. I grafted and it paid dividends. I felt this most keenly when I was presenting my Sunday morning show on Radio 5 Live, looking ahead to the week in sport and realising how much I knew. I also loved working alongside Chessie again. I think this job gave me the most satisfaction as it brought so many threads of my life together. I recognise a similar sense of satisfaction when I see my kids throw themselves into their sporting interests. It's a family affair.

16

Who Dares Wins

'It wasn't about winning for me;
it was about surviving without falling apart.'

If there was ever a show made for me, it was *Celebrity SAS: Who Dares Wins.* They invited me to take part and it came along at just the right time. I had hit a difficult point in my life and I felt very stuck, like I was sitting at the top of a water slide trying to decide which chute to go down. From hard-won experience, I knew I needed to challenge myself to remind me I could cope with whatever was thrown my way. I know it may sound like an unconventional approach, but, as I have explained, it had worked for me in the past. I had solved emotional hurt by finding something physically painful to distract me, so why not try it again? It was time to prove to myself I could be in tough situations, stay in control and emerge triumphant. Who dares wins, right?!

Off I went to a remote island in the Scottish Highlands for a fortnight, with a cracking group of celebrities and the kick-ass SAS team. As a fan of the show, I thought I knew what I was letting myself in for and was ready to be put through my paces. I was in my element running up and down mountains carrying logs, falling out of helicopters into icy lochs and being in the mess with the rest of the contestants. I loved it and would happily do it again, which I know will sound weird considering what I am going to say next. Unsurprisingly, the experience was also much harder than it looks on telly.

As I have already mentioned, as well as the physical effort, there were regular mental hurdles to overcome, like a severe lack of sleep and a deep insecurity about what was going to happen next. Those things combined with the regular interrogations almost had me at breaking point, which is exactly what they are designed to do. I had two allies who bolstered me at different points. The first was TV presenter Anthea Turner, whom I had met several times before and hugely admired. As we were sent on yet another mystery mission without any idea what we would be required to do, she reminded me we could handle this because we came from the *Blue Peter* school of excellence. We were already trained in being thrown into all sort of different situations at the last minute and having to survive them on camera. She tapped her head with her finger and said, 'Remember, they can only get to you in here if you let them. Don't let them. We know what we have achieved before.' It was exactly what I needed to hear.

My second support was the actress Nikki Sanderson. What a remarkable woman she is. She got me through the experience. While several of the group were breaking down in the interrogations, we remained stoic and silent. They dug around for our demons but we kept quiet. Neither of us were there to share them. Yes, it's good to talk, but is it *always* good to talk?! The show is designed to break you so I wanted to try to avoid that happening. It wasn't about winning for me; it was about surviving without falling apart.

There are situations that can't be properly portrayed on screen. It is impossible to see how little sleep we had or understand that we were always on edge. We could be told to grab our stuff, sent out to the parade ground, pushed into Land Rovers with bags pulled over our heads and driven around for an hour. During that time, we would be psyching ourselves up for what was to come. Then, when the bags came off, we found ourselves back at the parade ground. Nothing had happened. We could be taken to a jetty and made to stand teetering on the edge looking into the water before being turned around and taken back again. When we were in the mess, we wouldn't take our boots off for fear we would be summoned outside in full kit. I would delay crossing the courtyard to go to the toilet block because as soon as I did I was scared they would shout for us to be on the parade square, and a missing contestant meant all contestants were made to do five hundred burpees.

Every night, we took it in turns to guard from the watchtower. The rota was in pairs in two-hour intervals, so once you had done your stint you would return to the others to wake up the next couple. I did it with the dancer Brendan Cole, who was great fun, but at 3am we would have both preferred to be asleep. Towards the end, when there was a much smaller group left, we would barely be back in bed before we were up again for our next shift. Food was also used against us. We were always hungry and who knew if we would get a boiled egg or a spoonful of rice?

It was also difficult to tell on screen how intimidating the SAS guys were. They were scary and there was no respite. They were constantly trying to press my buttons, but I knew I had to stand firm because otherwise I would lose it, and not in a good way. I didn't want to talk about my personal life or unravel in front of Ant Middleton. I think the production team were respectful about how they edited the show, but I didn't want to test the theory. Coming from a TV background, I was very conscious of how things would look, what context it was being put in and how it would be cut. We were miked and hidden cameras followed our every move so there was no escape. Every minute in that environment is recorded, relevant and interpreted. I didn't drop my guard but it was so hard because it required more mental stamina than the physical challenges. I would be sitting with one of the group who may be pouring their heart out about something and part of me would be listening and reassuring, but the other part would be very aware of being watched. I wanted to warn them to remember the cameras.

Nikki felt the same as me. We had both been in the industry a long time and given a lot of ourselves. We didn't want to give everything. On a show like this one, you do better and probably get more out of it if you can let your guard down but I couldn't risk it at the time. I was so proud of those who did, like footballer and presenter John Fashanu, who spoke movingly about his brother's suicide, and TV personality Joey Essex, who opened up about the death of his mother. I applaud them for their bravery and honesty.

There was one interrogation that almost pushed me over the edge. I talked about it earlier in the book, but it was the accusation that I had been a dangerous flirt in my youth, pitching men against each other. They accused me of manipulation and it was deeply wounding. I was faced with one of the worst things someone has ever said about me. I just about managed to hold it together. Which is doubly hard on two hours' sleep, a boiled egg and day of being dropped into rivers. By this point I wasn't sure I knew my own name, let alone anything about my psychological profile.

I was in the series until the last ten minutes. The reason I didn't win was because I refused to give the SAS guys the names of my teammates and everyone else, apart from Nikki, blabbed. Which you would think would make us the undisputed champions, but the point was to stay alive and so divulging information at the right time to save myself was key. Throughout the intense interrogation I would not budge, even when what I thought was hot coffee was thrown in my face. It turned out to be water although I didn't know that until it hit me. I didn't flinch and the instructors were like, 'She's either hard as nails or psycho!' I got 'shot' just before the end and Nikki and I shared third place. We went out with dignity, safe in the knowledge that we had not opened up about anything we weren't comfortable discussing. I remember one of the production team coming up to me afterwards and saying, 'We nearly broke you.' Nearly, but not quite. So I guess the ultimate victory was mine.

17

Strictly Life Saver

*'This was me standing up straight
and putting on my invisible crown.'*

I joined *Strictly Come Dancing* at the last minute. There were several reasons why I thought about turning it down. Elsie was only six months old; my boys were at primary school in Leeds; I had my Radio 5 Live show and my husband had left me.

I was in shock. I know that following break-ups, people often say they didn't see it coming and it sounds like such a cliché, but that was me. Maybe I was consumed by the children, work, the renovation on a house we had just bought together. Recently having another baby and being now parents to three, despite all the exhaustion that entails, was what we had both wanted, planned and worked towards. Maybe there were signs and I missed them, or chose to ignore them. I will always have questions from that chapter of my life. There are moments that don't make sense, and conversations and exchanges with friends that create more questions than answers. But they aren't questions to which the answers will ever bring me peace. Facts are facts. He was gone.

It took me a while to build up the courage to tell my parents that my marriage had fallen apart. It's not a pain you want to inflict on those who love you most, nor is it an admission you want to make or a reality you want to face. After a few weeks of late nights with the baby, chaotic school runs and my new reality starting to dawn, it was all taking its toll and my friends could see something was up. They just had to look at my face to know, and their own faces were full of concern and care. One pal popped over and cried when she saw me holding Elsie. My friends were just as gobsmacked by this turn of events as I was. I had good people in my school mum circle, and the kindness of my 'al fresco wine group' carried me through some difficult weeks. One day, my dad arrived at my door on a 'detour' from work – they lived two hours away so it was a hell of a detour. He knew I was on my own with three small children, but I hadn't told my parents exactly what was going on as I didn't want to upset them. He immediately stepped in, knowing I needed him even though I didn't want to admit it.

Since then, my parents have always been by my side, doing all the things I am about to forget, like buying milk, sorting out uniforms, putting the bins out and helping with homework. I wouldn't have got through the initial few months without them so I wanted to find a way to show my appreciation. I messaged one of the *Strictly* production team who I knew and asked if I could get tickets for the 2022 series as a thank you to Mum, who loved the show. She replied and said, 'Yes, but do you want to be in it?' And I wrote, 'Ha, ha, good one.' It turned out she wasn't joking.

A Zoom chat was arranged with show's celebrity producer, Stefania Aleksander, and the executive producer, Sarah James. Beforehand, I fed Elsie, put her in the back of the car and did the classic 'I'll go for a drive so the baby naps and I can make a call in peace' manoeuvre. I got a takeaway coffee and sat in the front of the car while Elsie slept in the back. Talking to them both was instantly reassuring as they understood the juggle of work and parenting responsibilities. Sarah also had a little girl so I felt her empathy and protectiveness of my situation. Our conversation ranged from 'it's a big commitment', to 'how could we make it work?', to 'is this a ridiculous idea?' to 'we think you should do it'.

We all gave ourselves twenty-four hours to think. They went away and talked to the telly bosses and I drove round to my friend Carolynne's house and we wrestled with the idea. She is a close friend of our family, an unquestionable strength in my life, and had already suggested *Strictly* was exactly what I should be doing. She and Rebecca had been at my house at bedtimes, watching me do baths and tea for three under six, helping me with food shops and holding the baby while I navigated life admin and work responsibilities. At times, they were as hurt by what was happening in my life as I was.

Carolynne was adamant I should do it. I think at one point she even said, 'If you don't make it happen, I will.' My Caz isn't the kind of woman you mess with. Everyone has times when real-life noise is so deafening it's hard to make a rational decision. You don't know what is best for you and in those moments you hope you have friends and family who can support and guide you.

The list of pros and cons was long. It offered financial security at a nerve-wracking time; it would be a distraction and it was the biggest show on telly. That said, I had just taken a very public emotional battering. Elsie was so small but I reasoned she was still at the age where she would have big naps and wouldn't know. My mum had just retired and wanted to help more. It was something positive, exciting and different, so she did what all good mums do and told me to go for it. It would distract me for a few weeks and then I would be back with my kids, feeling happier. I couldn't imagine lasting until the end so I didn't think about the potential of it being a four-month commitment.

I hated people looking at me with pity, like I was an abandoned puppy, as I tried to navigate the very public break-up. People would ask if I was OK and I would have to reply, 'Yeah, I'm OK.' When in fact the truth would be too hard for me to say or for them to hear. *Strictly* offered me a chance to change that conversation; it would make my year about something other than the breakdown of my marriage and give my family and friends something to be proud of. The show would be noisy enough to block out the bad stuff. I said yes.

Once it was confirmed, I spoke to a few more friends about it. The reaction this time was one of barely disguised horror. My best mates said people who have been dumped go to Ibiza for a mad weekend, snog someone they shouldn't, relax on a juice retreat, get a haircut or take up a new hobby. They do not go on one of the biggest shows on television. I talked to work pals who were also *Strictly* alumni, like Dan Walker, Gethin Jones and Ore Oduba. They said 'Really?' with that look friends give when they think this is quite possibly the worst idea you have ever had. Dan told me not to underestimate how emotionally exposing the experience would be. Was this really the right time to do it? It was likely to fuel the press too. My private life had been plastered over the papers all summer so I just thought, *What's another few months?* I was numb and immune to the coverage by then. I really valued Dan's opinion because he had been through it and he was watching out for me, but a gut instinct – or a sudden madness –made me accept the job. Considering how far my life had unravelled, I should have taken some time out, but I went into *Strictly* instead. It turned out to be the best thing I ever did.

At the beginning of *Strictly,* I had to go down to London for a day to meet the rest of the celebrities, dancers and production team. I had left the kids with a childminder back home in Leeds and I felt miserable on the train. What the hell was I doing? How did I think I could make this work? Tony Adams, the legend, turned up in a t-shirt that said, 'Sorry I'm late, I didn't want to be here.' And that summed it up for me in that moment. Within a short time of being in the studio I had poured my heart out to fellow contestant Kaye Adams and talent producer Jasmine Fox, like I had known them for years.

'Get your mum on board,' Jasmine reassured me, knowing full well if you're lucky enough to have a mum like mine, you don't panic when you're not with your kids. That anxiety of them being away from you is neutralised by the knowledge that Granny is in charge and they'll be having a good time while you have to work. I have been lucky that I have had lots of time off with my boys; I never had to get a nanny or formal childcare because we could always balance it. There were moments when I had been stuck in the run-up to *Strictly*. Like the time I dashed to hospital with Ernie, who had broken his toe, and had to ask a Rugby League friend to look after the other two at home. Or when I was presenting Channel 4's *Steph's Packed Lunch,* the kids' school shut and I had twenty-six missed calls on my phone. My parents were on the contact list but they were two hours away. There was no back-up. And I knew I couldn't attempt *Strictly* without proper support.

Everyone suggested I went back to Cumbria for a while. I agonised over it. I had to ask myself some honest questions. Was doing *Strictly* a selfish decision? If I didn't do *Strictly,* could we stay in Leeds? Or was I using *Strictly* as an excuse to move back to the support network of family and friends and an idyllic rural lifestyle? I didn't want to uproot the kids considering the change already happening in their little lives, but heading home to Cumbria felt like the only answer. I talked about it with them and they weren't sure about leaving their school, so I took them on a playdate with my friend and her kids who went to the local village school back home. They all got on really well. Ernie said to me, 'Mum, we will try that school if you want.' He made my heart burst with his understanding of the situation. As long as I reassured him he would be in a football team that played proper matches, he was willing to give it a go. I have had some very difficult conversations with my boys and it's not something I would wish on any parent. No one wants to tell their children they aren't getting the fairy tale. If you're navigating it, I hope it goes with as few tears as possible for everyone involved.

I had previous form with *Strictly* because I'd taken part in the Christmas special ten years before. I was filming a holiday series at the same time so I only had four intensive days to train, rather than the allotted two weeks. At the opening titles shoot, I realised that everyone had learned their dance apart from me. I had dashed away from my day job to come to the studio and get kitted out in a push-up silver bra, sparkly skirt and massive ponytail. My dance partner for the special, Artem Chigvintsev, picked me up, spun me around and laid me across popstar JB Gill's knee. JB was dressed as a tin soldier. At which point, Kristina Rihanoff shouted, 'CUT!' and said, 'Helen, you look really confused!' I was. I couldn't quite get my head around what I was doing and why I was there. It felt like I had been transported into another world, which, in a way, I had.

Artem and I worked really well together because we were both driven. I could train for eleven hours a day and he loved that. On the first day of training, Pasha Kovalev popped his head around the studio door to ask if he could borrow Artem when we took a break. He wanted him to look at a dance he was choreographing for Kimberley Walsh, who was in the final of the main show. I said jokingly, 'Whoa, Pasha, we don't take breaks!' Artem said, 'This is why I love you!' To which I replied, 'I was kidding! We do take breaks, yes?' This was when I realised those dancers were grafters.

Despite this brief encounter with the *Strictly* machine, in 2022 I was not as prepared as I should have been for the glitz and glamour of the ballroom. My first hint of this was when I did an interview with the *Brood* magazine editor Tom Pitfield. He is married to actress and *Strictly* alumni Catherine Tyldesley, so he knew a lot about how the show worked. At the end, I asked him to take a quick photo of me on my phone as *Strictly* needed a headshot. He thought I was joking. Apparently, that was the sort of thing I should have had hair, make-up and a professional photographer for. I was clueless. Tom was not, and took a peach of a shot.

Before we left Leeds to move back to Cumbria, I filmed the title shoot and the dance partner meeting for *Strictly*. My life was so chaotic at this point that I rocked up with Louis, baby Elsie and my dog. Luckily, Ernie was at a football camp, so that was one less thing to worry about. This was my first day on the biggest show in telly and I was still naïvely thinking I could do it all. I asked the bemused runner to push the pram and gave her a tennis ball to throw for the boy and the dog while I did the interview. I still have a photo of her with my kids, dog and the harassed Talent Executive, Steff Aleksander, who had come up from London for what she thought was a five-hour shoot, but I had just told her it was going to be two hours because I had to collect Ernie. If that isn't the epitome of the working mum juggle then I don't know what is. We all laughed about it later. Not at the time, though. At the time, I felt a bit sick and seriously questioned what the hell I was doing.

This was also the day I met Gorka Márquez, my professional dance partner. Our introduction was filmed and I was supposed to run and jump into the arms of this bloke I had never met. I felt so awkward about it because I am just not that sort of person. Gorka and I have become such good friends – I love the bones of him – but I wouldn't even do it now. It's not very me. It was an awkward moment in the park, with one eye on the kids and the other on the clock so I wasn't late for Ernie. I was really excited to be dancing with Gorka and grateful to be part of the whole thing, but I was nervous. There was a lot going on, I wasn't myself and I wasn't sure I had the capacity to deal with everything this new challenge was going to throw at me. I had quite the battle ahead with that. I was also worried Gorka would be disappointed to be paired up with the middle-aged, dumped, depressed one crying into her wine every five minutes!

I was not a bruised bride and I didn't want him to think he had pulled the short straw.

On the first day of the September school term, we moved back to Cumbria and into the spare room at my parents' house while I was on *Strictly*. Leaving Leeds and the family home we had spent a couple of years renovating was discombobulating. I couldn't get my head around it. The saving grace was my cousin's best friend, Helena, who had become my Girl Friday in the aftermath of Richie leaving. Funnily enough, teenage me had babysat her when she was tiny and our dads played golf together so there were strong family connections. Now there she was, helping me through one of the worst times of my life. Towards the end of *Strictly,* Helena packed everything up for me, she oversaw the movers and she unpacked it all in the rental I had found in a village near my parents. She was an absolute star. When I walked into the house she had posted yellow sticky notes everywhere saying what was in cupboards and drawers so I could find things quickly. She even stocked up a drawer with useful items like batteries and matches. It was a lifesaver. I'm telling you, there's a generation of women who need a Helena. It was like the bit in *And Just Like That . . .* when Carrie gets the girl from St Louis to pack up her apartment after her husband dies. Not for the first time, my friends compared me to Carrie – although this is due to our shared ability to make chaotic and emotionally bad decisions rather than for an appreciation of fine shoes.

Just like all the challenges I have done, I went into *Strictly* with naïve optimism. I mean, hello! It's dancing, how hard could it be compared to running three marathons in a day?! Oh, how wrong I was. It wasn't just the level of physical fitness needed that surprised me but the vulnerability I felt. The first few days of training were like an out-of-body experience where I looked down on myself, awkward and graceless, dancing with a complete stranger.

Our first dance was the American Smooth to Aretha Franklin's 'You Send Me'. It was beautiful. Or at least, it would have been, had Gorka been dancing with a professional partner. I couldn't shake the feeling of being completely out of my depth. I had to sit at a piano and Gorka gently tipped my chin to get my attention. He said every time he did it, he thought I was going to slap him! I knew it was the dance but it felt inappropriate. In my world, it wasn't normal to have my face stroked by someone I wasn't romantically involved with and I am not a face stroker even then. In the same dance, Gorka had me in a ballroom hold and then lifted me up in the air. Me, a thirty-nine-year-old woman who had just had a kid! Was I alright about that? Not really. I also had to pretend to write notes on a piece of paper as if I was writing a song. For some reason, I found it mortifying. I literally couldn't do it, I was so embarrassed. 'But I am not actually writing on the paper, am I?' I asked. 'Yes,' Gorka replied. That turned out to be the easy part.

Ashley, one of the choreographers, popped in to check how we were doing and wanted to see the dance. I couldn't do it. I was too terrified to show her so Gorka took control. He said, 'Ashley is here to help. She's on your side and also, newsflash, you are doing this dance for twelve million people on Saturday. If you can't do it for one then we have a serious problem.' I did the dance for her and it was awful, awful, awful! I knew I was doomed.

After an intense week, I turned up at the studio on Friday for rehearsals. Now, I love live TV and big, shiny-floored studios; I never fail to feel excited. I also know a lot of people because I have been around a long time, so it was lovely to be back working with old crew from previous programmes, like Chris who I first worked with at *Blue Peter* and who was now head of cameras for *Strictly*. When I had the kids I made a conscious decision to step back from this world. Not away from it forever, but to stay on the edge of it, and I focused on work that would fit around the family. Doing *Strictly* put me back into my world and I was so happy to be there. But I had lost my nerve.

I went out on to the dance floor for the rehearsal before the main show and I was so petrified that I couldn't move. All

I had to do was perform it for the choreographers and cameras. I don't know what came over me, but I ran and hid on the fire escape. Gorka was perplexed, but not as much I was. I had jumped out of a helicopter backwards and fallen head-first into a freezing Scottish lake for goodness' sake, yet I couldn't step on to a dance floor, hold his hand and spin around for a couple of minutes. That was all I had to do. My confidence was non-existent. I couldn't even hold a normal conversation in that room. I no longer recognised myself.

It was a heart-sinking moment. I stood on the fire escape and thought, *I can't do this*. There had been a lot of personal stuff to wade through in the week. I had been upbeat and jolly with Gorka because I wanted him to think I was fun to be around, so I hadn't shared the reality. On the fire escape we had a bit of a breakthrough. Gorka said he couldn't help me if I didn't let him. 'Tell me what's going on,' he said, so I did. Bless him, to this day I am not sure if he is glad he asked. Still, it worked and I got through the rehearsal, then the night of the live show went past in an intense blur. I was relieved to have got the first one out of the way without falling over or throwing up.

In week two, Gorka asked me why I didn't feel sexy. It was an awkward question that immediately made me cringe. Why ask me that?! I was just there for the banter. I have never been sexy;

I was the cute, funny type. Gorka put mirrors up around me and suggested I dance around and make myself feel good. Was he mad?! It was like turning my skin inside out. I had to push through a high level of discomfort. He was asking a woman with three children under six, whose husband of ten years had left her and was with another woman, TO BE SEXY. I thought, *Who would feel good about themselves in that scenario?!*

Our second dance was the cha-cha, to Lady Gaga and Ariana Grande's 'Rain on Me', and it was very flirty and sexual. Yet again, it was mortifying. Even now I can't listen to that song without coming out in a cold sweat. I tried to visualise being in a club and making eyes at a guy, like Gorka told me to, but I was never that girl, even in my youth. After being in a relationship for a long time, it was strange to be single and I wasn't sure who I was or how to behave around men. I was not the kind of woman to embrace sexy dancing. It was uncomfortable and I suspect it was frustrating for Gorka because we had no time to navigate my awkwardness.

Going into *Strictly*, I already knew Gorka's partner, Gemma Atkinson, through friends who had done the show before. She was cut from the same cloth as me and told me how she'd had to do a rhumba when she was on the show and had felt incredibly uncomfortable. Thank the Lord it wasn't just me. I knew she understood and I think she helped Gorka to as well. He wanted me to do well; he was passionate and invested, and

I felt that from the beginning. I didn't want to let him down, but we both had to learn early on not to be too serious and we weren't. It's always been important to me in any situation to laugh more than you cry, and with Gorka there were a lot of laughs.

In the first few weeks of *Strictly*, I felt like a little girl trying to walk around in her mum's shoes or an athlete having to wear heels after a lifetime in trainers. It just didn't feel right. The more I tried to be sexy, the worst it felt. The judges said I looked like I was second-guessing myself all the time and they were bang on. It was like they could see into my soul. Gorka quickly learned how to deal with me. Of course, there were intense moments but we never left on an argument. There were always kind words and jokes. Of the many plaudits I could give him, one of his best qualities was being quick to acknowledge if he had mishandled a conversation and to take accountability. He was also strict, which was the kick up the bum I needed. If he had been softly, softly, nicey, nicey, I don't think I would have got as far as I did.

I spent the second live show with my heart in my mouth. I was relieved not to be the first one to leave but gutted to lose my friend Kaye, who is one of the most quickwitted women I have ever met.

* * *

The third week was Movie Week and we performed the Viennese waltz to 'Hopelessly Devoted to You' from the *Grease* soundtrack. It was hilarious because it was so ironic. I was in the middle of a very public break-up and this was the song they had chosen for me. Gorka coached me on my emotional performance of the dance by instructing me to think about something really sad, then listed a few things to get me in the zone. I was like, 'Wow, alright mate, I get it!' And he said, 'Have I gone too far?' And I said, 'Yes, unless you've got Prosecco and you can crank up Taylor Swift, stop talking.'

After my initial reticence, I loved the training. I could be in the training room for nine hours a day, no problem. The sucker punch was stepping out on to the dance floor. I didn't understand how it could be so hard. I have had a career in a multi-camera environment so I know what I am doing, but as soon as I was directed to milk the cameras, I just couldn't. I would go back to my dressing room and wonder why I was loving the experience but also feeling that it was just so wrong?

In fairness, I wasn't used to being on camera in a sparkly bra. Or getting a spray tan – Venetian plaster or biscuit beige?! Lisa Davey, head of hair, and Lisa Armstrong, head of make-up, were divine and bent over backwards to make me look and feel special. I was so far away from who I was, and certainly from who I had become in recent months, that I couldn't shake the uncomfortable feeling that I may be making a complete fool of myself. One of the hair team, Anna, would see my fear and chant, 'You're amazing' before I went on. The team also knew I couldn't stay still for long, so rather than planning something complicated that would take three hours, they tried to get me done in twenty minutes. They would say, 'Helen, you look sensational!' and I would say, 'Do I? Or do I look like a tit?!' Once, I was dressed as a gypsy wench in a busty top with flowers in my hair and Ellie Taylor was dressed as Little Bo Peep. She took one look at me and she said, 'We've got mortgages. We are supposed to be grown-ups.' And I said, 'I know, what are we doing?!' Secretly we loved it, even though we were more out of our comfort zones than some of the others.

The real reason I loved going into hair, make-up and wardrobe was to hang out with the wonderful people there. Many of them had kids and understood how hard I found it to leave mine behind. One particularly tough morning, Vicky Gill, the head of wardrobe, linked her arm in mine; she didn't have to ask anything, she just knew. She has three children too. 'This is OK,' she said. 'We like our jobs and we like our kids. The two things can co-exist. You don't love them any less.' I felt totally seen. On several occasions when I went into wardrobe, Vicky could sense I was overwhelmed and she would tell me to sit under her desk for five minutes. I hid quietly out of sight to collect myself. In many ways, being thrust into this huge show with incredible people was like a form of therapy, in which I was supported by others who had been through tough times and come out the other side. I laughed a lot, especially with assistant producer, Joe Wheatley. I got something from each of them and I didn't realise it but, bit by bit, they were putting me back together.

On the live show in the third week we were the penultimate couple to go on, so I was beside myself by the time we went out on to the floor. Amazingly, we got good scores from the judges but that didn't guarantee a safe place through to the next week. The dance-off was between Fleur East and Richie Anderson. They had become good friends of mine so it was painful to watch. Richie went that week. He is one of the most gracious and grateful people I have ever worked with, with an energy and kindness which everyone could, and did, feed off.

The fourth week was the paso doble to Rodrigo y Gabriela's 'Tamacun' and Gorka was firing on all cylinders. He wanted to inject authentic flamenco into the piece, which meant pushing himself beyond his limit. He spoke to a friend in Spain and had a proper flamenco lesson. He said nobody had done flamenco on *Strictly* and if anyone could then I could. No pressure, then. Neither of us could have predicted what happened next.

I'd just heard via friends that my husband was having a baby.

Days later, the *Sun* confirmed it with a front-page spread and a photo of me. It's hard to say more because there are personal and private consequences to consider, but it wasn't easy. My week went from tough to almost unbearable and then I had to go on live television on Saturday night, dressed as a Spanish wench, and tap-dance on a box. The judges' reaction was about owning it, being more confident and selling the dance. They said I looked good but I danced like I was scared of my own shadow. I got a six from Craig and Gorka was furious. I did think the fact I was even on the dance floor was an achievement. I hadn't taken to my bed. I was not waist-deep in gin. I was there, attempting to dance flamenco in front of the nation. I didn't say anything. Yet, this is one of the best lessons I learned during *Strictly*. In the nicest possible way, when it comes to the dance, nobody cares what is going on in your personal life, and that's as it should be. Should they have said, 'Helen, that wasn't very good, but you've had a shit week so we will give you a ten'?! No. They should not.

In Claudia's area afterwards, Gorka surprised me during the interview with, 'Can I just say something?' which has since become one of our catchphrases. On camera, he said, 'I know you have been having a difficult time and you may not feel like you are good enough or beautiful. Even if you don't believe in yourself, I believe in you, your family believe in you. Everyone here believes in you.' At which point, the assembled dancers cheered and Claudia shouted, 'We all believe in you!' and I tried to hide behind Gorka's back. He continued, 'It doesn't matter how many times anyone else tells you to believe in yourself, it's only you who can make the change. You are an amazing woman, mother and incredible dancer, so believe in yourself please.' More cheers followed.

Ninety per cent of me wanted the ground to swallow me up. I was dying inside and wished he would shut up. The other ten per cent wanted to hug Gorka for what he had said. It was so wrong, but so right. He knew how much I was dealing with and saw every time my phone pinged with tricky messages or I had to dash to get back for the kids. I was so embarrassed by his speech I jumped on the table and did an ole-style flamenco move in a bid to distract everyone. I just didn't know how to respond to what he had said so I thought it may be the only way to make him stop!

We went through to the next week and said a sad goodbye to Matt Goss, a man with more life experience than ten men put together and one of the kindest hearts I have ever crossed paths with.

Social media was full of Gorka's speech the following day and he was turned into a gif. He was even trending on Twitter, so much so that one of Gemma's friends thought he had died! Should he have said it? No, probably not. Am I glad he said it? Yes, I am. I wasn't talking about my private life on camera and it wasn't his story to tell, but he went for it and I could see he had my back. It came from the best place. He wasn't saying it to keep me in the competition; he genuinely wanted everyone to understand what it had taken for me to turn up and dance that week. I know my friends were happy that he had spoken out. There was an assumption that I would share more on camera about the effect my marriage break-up was having on me but I couldn't go there. I felt the ever-protective presence of the executive producer Sarah, too, who was like a close girlfriend on a night out, making sure I didn't make a fool of myself. That evening was a significant milestone in my friendship with Gorka and, from that moment, after having his say, he didn't speak about it in public again.

Week five was the BBC's centenary celebration, which coincided with a massive personal breakthrough when we performed the Charleston to the *Blue Peter* theme tune. During training, an external choreographer came in and picked up on how Gorka would encourage me to 'own' the dance. She said he needed to explain what that meant because I wasn't a dancer so I couldn't understand. All credit to Gorka – he took that on board and worked on his direction, which really helped me develop. I had also taken Gorka to the *Blue Peter* studios and it reminded me how much I had done in my career, so why was I bothered about dancing? In that job, barely a week would have gone by without me jumping out of a plane. That Saturday night was the first time we opened the show. When we were on the stairs waiting to go on, Gorka was nervous. I hadn't seen him like that before; he usually did a really good job of hiding it. 'It's just like jumping out of a plane,' he said, grinning. And that was another catchphrase that stuck. Each week we would say to each other, 'We just have to jump out of the plane.'

After each live performance, during the applause, my instinct was to ask Gorka if it was OK, but he said that was the worst thing to do. Just jump around and pretend it's amazing. That's what owning it meant! I found that hard because I am my own worst critic so I was constantly looking for reassurance. However, I knew the Charleston had gone well because the judges were on their feet. Shirley stayed standing and said she was making a point because the week before they had told me I wasn't confident enough and now I had bossed it. God, that felt good.

My mindset was shifting and I realised that *Strictly* was a bit like being in Disneyland. Everyone is there to make you feel good, from the dancers to the choreographers to hair, make-up and wardrobe, and I was beginning to lean in to it. I started to trust the process and enjoy it more. I was no longer waking at 4am in a state of high anxiety. We were lucky with our

Charleston and got great scores, but Jayde Adams and Karen Heuer weren't and I hated saying goodbye to that pair. These two are the kind of friends every girl needs in her life.

My weekly schedule was intense, with training from Monday to Thursday in Cumbria or Lancaster, near where Gorka lived. I did as many drop-offs and pick-ups as I could with the kids before heading down to London for rehearsal and show days. My parents were amazing and doing all the legwork so I could swoop in to do the fun stuff. I had my Radio 5 Live show every Sunday morning too. The combination of work, travel and family responsibilities was mind-blowing. Yet, through much of it, I had Gorka by my side. We had a running joke that he would want me to take the easier option and do it well, and I would always want to push myself to the harder level and take the gamble. Apart from when I bottled the one-handed cartwheel.

We aren't the kind of people to gush about each other but if I was going to sing anyone's praises it would be his. We grew into our friendship and I was acutely aware that each week could be the last. He gave me my confidence back and this was cemented by the British public voting to keep me in the competition. In training, Gorka would point to his face and say, 'I know this doesn't look like I am happy, but I am very happy.'

His default position was that I could always do better but it didn't mean that I wasn't doing well. I think our partnership brought out good stuff in each other. He definitely brought out the best in me. I believe people come into our lives at the right time for the right reasons, and this was true of Gorka.

Halloween week was next, which was the foxtrot in the style of Little Red Riding Hood to a song of the same name by Sam the Sham and the Pharaohs. For this, I needed to act scared. I had spent weeks learning how *not* to look scared and now I had to do it for the dance. When I finished, Motsi said she was getting 'final vibes' and for the first time I allowed myself to think, *Maybe I do deserve to be here.* To use the old running analogy, if I was putting in all this effort it seemed a bit daft to run a half marathon, why not a full one?!

Everyone had stepped up their dancing game and it was exciting to see how well we were all doing at the halfway point of the competition. Neither Fleur nor James Bye should have been in the dance-off, but there they were and James left. He was the sort of man that everyone wanted to be around and he brought joy into every room.

The press interest continued. Every year there is a feverish debate about which Strictly contestants had previous dance experience. It was true that I had taken part in *Let's Dance for Comic Relief* in 2009 and the *Strictly Christmas Special* in 2012, performing one dance in each. It was categorically untrue that

I had been a qualified tap dance teacher when I was younger. This credit had weirdly appeared on my Wikipedia page, which meant it was then picked up by a researcher on a Saturday morning show and repeated by the presenter James Martin. To refute it on live TV felt embarrassing, but I should have done because the inaccuracy didn't go away. Neither did stories about my life off the dance floor.

Even my own mum would get confused by ambiguous headlines and misconstrued stories. She saw an article saying, 'Helen opens up about single life' and questioned whether I should be talking about it. 'Mum,' I said, 'read the article. It's just a picture of me walking the dog and a rehashed quote from a year ago.' In the middle of *Strictly*, Mum had seen something online and asked, 'What were you doing in Nando's last night with Will Mellor?' And I said, 'Where was I last night, Mum?' 'Oh, you were with me.' So there you go. Even Dad got a taste of it. He was down at the golf club and his friends mentioned a piece they had read about my growing success in *Strictly*. 'So we see your Helen's worth £6 million then,' they said. 'Is she?' Dad replied. 'Because if she is then why is she sleeping in my back bedroom with her three kids? She better start paying some keep.'

Week seven was the jive. When we practised, Gorka was quite

the taskmaster, which worked for me because I like to push myself fitness wise. We were relentlessly doing a particular step and the perspiration was running down his nose. As he was shouting 'One, two, one, two,' he spat the sweat into my face and then apologised. I told him to keep going. Afterwards, he said that was when he knew we were cut from the same cloth because I didn't flinch.

We danced the jive to Janelle Monáe's 'Tightrope' and I didn't have to be sexy. Like with the Charleston, when I did the jive in rehearsals the other dancers said, 'That's great,' and it was a little vote of confidence. You train in a bubble all week and have no idea if it's OK because you have no reference point or anyone telling you. I got a wonderful reaction on the night, which made it a very special moment and I felt like I had finally got into my stride. I had lost my identity somewhere along the way and then I was thrust into the *Strictly* world of sparkle, music and celebrity. Who was I? What did I bring the table? Now, I was beginning to think I had something to offer. I felt valued.

The judges scores totalled thirty-seven and Anton gave me my first ten, which was a massive boost. Craig was going to give me ten, but he pointed out a tiny mistake I had made right in front of him. What he didn't know was why I hadfaltered. I did a cartwheel and thought I was going to wet myself on live telly. In rehearsals, I had made the move and come a-cropper so I was nervous the same thing would happen again. To compensate, I did an extra big cartwheel to make sure I had enough power to get me through and as I came upright, I thought, as only a mother of an eight-month-old who had two kids already can think, *Oh God, I may wee.* Thankfully, I was wearing black and I managed to avert disaster even though I lost a point for it. I think that point was worth losing considering the alternative. I told Gorka I thought I was going to wet myself out there and he said, 'Yeah me too, I was so nervous.' And I said, 'Oh mate, you have no idea.' That week, we kept Molly Rainford, but lost lovely Ellie Simmonds in the dance-off. The girl with a twinkle in her eye.

Crunch time. Week eight was the salsa to Luis Fonsi, Daddy Yankee and Justin Bieber's 'Despacito' and a place in Blackpool was at stake. This was the stage in the process I had wanted to get to. I wanted to dance in the famous ballroom and then whatever happened from then, I would just be happy to have banked the experience. It wasn't a great dance. I had to stick on a wig and be sexy, and I still wasn't good at that. Gorka would say, 'Come on, you're an attractive woman!' And I would respond, 'I hear you, but you are making me feel uncomfortable even saying that.' I kept thinking, *I've got to do the school run next week.*

There is nothing worse than someone saying 'be sexy'. It's

harder than someone saying, 'be confident'. I can understand what confidence feels like and how to channel it but sexy is a different matter. Gorka is naturally sexy, it's like a dance move for him, but I didn't know how to mirror that. When someone tells you to be sexy and you already thought you were doing it then it's double agony! I wanted to be the woman who sashayed down the steps and shook her booty at a hot man, but it just wasn't me. I'm the woman standing on the side of a football pitch watching my sons play, usually the only mum in a group of ten dads. How could I face them after a provocative dance?! It would feel a bit like being a schoolteacher and then getting drunk at a bar on a Friday night in front of a group of my students' parents.

There are always rumours about flirtations and affairs in every series of *Strictly,* but just because everyone is sexy on the dance floor doesn't mean they behave like it behind the scenes. It's actually about physicality, it's not sexual. The dancers are professional athletes and they view their bodies in that way. Before a show, they would be in the long corridor outside the dressing rooms, often standing around in their boxer shorts, chatting about normal stuff while they stretched and lunged. To begin with, it was disconcerting to be surrounded by so many almost naked, perfect bodies; this behaviour wasn't normal for the world I was from. Yet, it was completely normal in theirs. I had no physical confidence and they made me feel strong because they looked at bodies in a different way, seeing pregnancy and childbirth as a powerful achievement. It was about how much the body could do, not what it looked like, and it made me relax. Several times I had to have the gusset of my knickers sewn into my costume while I was wearing it, so there were two people fussing around my crotch. I didn't bat an eyelid.

Despite all my reservations, we got through to Blackpool! Buoyed by a dance created by Ash and Arduino, two choreographers who saw and heard everything, and knew what to say at the right time. Tony Adams and Tyler West were in the bottom two, but Tony had a painful hamstring injury from his first performance, so couldn't dance again and pulled out. I was relieved that Tyler was coming with us to Blackpool and really sad Tony wasn't. Never did I expect to share so many stories and parenting tips with Tony Adams, and I have met up with him and his family regularly ever since the show. He's an education and a joy to be around.

I can't tell you how pleased I was to make it to Blackpool. I was desperate for my family to come and Blackpool was a much easier visit than making it all the way to Elstree. My children have always been to work with me and the chance for them to experience the wonder that is a live *Strictly* was pretty special. As a father, Gorka knew how much I was struggling spending long days away from the kids. Mum would bring them to training to see me because I wanted them to know where I was and what I was doing so they would be OK with it. It was strange to be doing this at a time when I had planned to be in baby groups, but instead I was in a dance studio and I beat myself up about that. Gorka said if everyone could see me coming back to myself each week then so could my kids. They saw me work hard with a smile on my face and I was becoming a better version of me for them. I couldn't really argue with that.

Gorka and I had talked about getting our families together should we make it to the home of ballroom, but we never really let ourselves think about it. Maybe it was that, maybe it was the relief of surviving so long into the competition, or the extra dancers that joined for that week, or maybe it was just being in the seaside town where I'd spent so many fun-filled family holidays, but Blackpool week was heaven and the dance clicked. I learned it all in the first couple of hours and that never happened. I was consumed by the dancing, the goodwill, the fabulous costumes and make-up, and the endorphins. We trained harder that week than we had ever trained. Gorka had me dance around the room holding a chair at shoulder height and we ran the routine again and again and again. He wanted me to hit that dance floor with confidence and I think I did.

My parents brought the children to the ballroom and I have

never felt so much pride. They had been staying up late to watch the show on television every week with their cousins, but now they had stepped into the screen, in among the lights, cameras, shiny floor and amazing dancers. Ernie played on a phone but Elsie and Louis were in awe and charmed the room. Most of my fellow contestants saw first-hand that I wasn't kidding when I had explained how energetic and fabulously feral my children were. The baby bounced from Fleur to Molly to Karen and Amy, while the boys told rude jokes to Giovanni and Nikita. The kids were in their element and so was I.

It was thrilling to have backing dancers, who filled the space at the Tower Ballroom and bolstered my energy and performance. I had to really embrace it otherwise I would be letting them down. We did the quickstep to Mark Ronson and Amy Winehouse's 'Valerie' and whipped around the dance floor at lightning speed. I will never forget Katya telling me to just scream, go for it and overdo the bravado. The team support was very heartfelt. The place erupted and so did we. Anton Du Beke kept talking about the atmosphere and the reaction, pointing out to me that's what you live for as a performer. I am not a performer but I felt like one that night.

We were so delirious in Claudia's area that we made no sense, which is frustrating because you really want to say the right thing, but your week has been building up to that dance and you can't process the response. I just babbled nonsense most weeks and I certainly did that at Blackpool. A good night turned into a great night as telly friends, family and school friends joined us for the after party. Keith Lemon was amused by the fact I was wearing walking boots, training gear and full *Strictly* make-up. I was living out of a bag so I was wearing whatever was clean and that was that at the time. Of all the precious memories from that night, the best one is, having watched me dancing at the party, chatting to everyone, enjoying the room, Dad saying he felt like he had seen me again. At the same moment, I think Gorka realised this wasn't just dancing for me. It was so much more.

The sting in the tail was seeing Molly and Tyler in the dance-off and then losing Tyler. I didn't want either of my friends to go. Tyler is like the kid brother everyone wants. Talented, kind and a gentleman. I still owe his mum dinner because I want to know what she did to raise such an amazing young man.

There were so many people who contributed to me finding myself. I used to cringe when TV contestants would gush about their 'family' but now I totally get it. I was surrounded by strong and brilliant people at exactly the moment I needed to be. From production and crew to the choreographers and professional dancers, like the wonderful, free-spirited Dianne Buswell, who said she kept bumping into people who wished me well, supportive Katya Jones, Luba Mushtuk with the best one-liners and Nikita Kuzmin, Vito Coppola, Carlos Gu, Kai

Widdrington and Graziano Di Prima who all made me feel like I was interesting and funny. Their kind words were perfectly timed. Johannes would say, 'Go slay, Mama!' as he passed. Each of the professional dancers blew my mind with their work ethic and commitment to each of us amateurs.

My fellow celebrities kept me going. I loved getting takeaways with them and sitting around the table chatting and comparing notes. Kym Marsh and I were probably the mums of the group and she would buy everyone a cocktail for their room or treat us to chocolates. Everyone would laugh at me because when we were in the green room, I would pick up all the cups as I went, like a maternal reflex.

One day, Mum sent a photo of a piece of homework Ernie had done. The school had asked him to say something about his mum and he wrote, 'My mum is brave.' I mentioned it to Ellie. She said, 'You *are* brave'. That's all she said, and it broke me.

We went from a big high to a bit of a low in week ten with the samba, performed to Emma Bunton's 'Eso Beso'. Gorka now knew not to push the sexy so we turned it into a comic routine, which was fun and also quite pivotal for me. I had got past Blackpool which had been my original target so every extra week was a bonus. I was just there to try my hardest, enjoy the night and get through the samba without being eliminated.

We scraped through but my dear pal Ellie Taylor didn't. I couldn't bear the idea that she and the fabulous Johannes Radebe wouldn't be hitting the dance floor together again, and I was going to miss Ellie desperately. Johannes is quite simply a higher being and in Ellie he found a match. It's rare to be that gorgeous, that funny, that kind-hearted and that emotionally intelligent, but she nails them all. She can also pull off the full routine to 'Stop' by the Spice Girls when she's a couple of gins deep.

And then, we were at week eleven. It was Musicals Week and we were given 'Mein Herr' from *Cabaret* for our Couple's Choice dance. In rehearsal, a renowned choreographer, Beth Honan, joined us. Gorka was excited to be working with her, so if he felt that way then I knew it was going to be special. I was drawn to the character of gritty survivor Sally Bowles, which also helped. Gorka knew what I was capable of and Beth knew how to make the most of it. She is one of those women who, when you meet her, you know has lived a life. Has seen some good times and some cruel souls. I didn't have to say anything to Beth, I just knew she got me. She had substance and I felt she saw some in me. We didn't have to talk about what the dance needed to say.

After the first day, we didn't have much to go on, then she came in the next morning triumphant. Standards were high and

Gorka was in his element. It was like being taken by your mum to see an aunt you had to impress, so every time Beth turned her back, Gorka would give me whispered notes about how to do it better. We didn't realise at the time that she clocked this and told someone we never took our feet off the pedal. It was a running joke that we didn't stop for food or TikTok filming. We danced till we dropped.

In the final rehearsal, Beth said to the supporting dancers, 'Right, Helen has got a moment every girl wants where she can say "fuck you", and not many people get the chance to do that, so let's make sure it works.' And all the dancers whooped in agreement. I got the costume on, did the rehearsal, went through the camera blocks and I just had a feeling. I thought, *I may just be able to pull this off.* To be something so alien to me was suddenly freeing. I was crawling around in suspenders, which was a far cry from where I had started all those weeks before. In this dance, I was in control. We had found a dance which let me own my moment and be the boss. Everything we had worked for came together in that dance. That was one of my most magic experiences on the series.

We did the live performance and the place went nuts. I mean: nuts. There was a buzz. I felt it and I thrived on it. Gorka had drilled me to stare into the camera. It wasn't something I had done in any of the other dances; usually, I was concentrating on the steps and technique. But this dance only worked if I locked eyes on the red light and didn't drop my gaze. It seemed to have the right effect. The reaction was big, in the room and online. I think people get a bit swept along with the excitement so I am sure the reaction was hyped up, but the fact that there was even a press piece dissecting the dance and the symbolic moments is testament to how it resonated with quite a few people.

The following day, my parents asked what all the fuss was about because they didn't know about the character of Sally Bowles. People read into it what they wanted. One of the dancers, with tears in her eyes, came up to me afterwards, swept me into her elegant embrace and said, 'You did that for all of us.'

We went into semi-finals without Kym, who had been voted out. She is one of the hardest-working, warmest women who I have the pleasure to call my friend. She was like a big sister, and when she and Graziano left we missed the energy they brought to the group. Semi-final week was tough for a lot of reasons. I had my radio show to do, my kids to get ready for a school week, and we were in the chaotic lead-up to Christmas. Plus, I had a week of filming for Channel 5's *This Week on the Farm,* the production team of which were characteristically supportive and brilliant, moving filming to later in the evening so we could train. They also welcomed Gorka to set. I hope he felt the love from my telly family as I did from his. The *Cabaret* performance had been costly for me privately because of an adverse reaction to it. Emotions on all sides were high. The fallout was tough to deal with. Up until the final, I regretted doing the dance but hindsight has made me realise that dance was about me. This was me standing up straight and putting on my invisible crown. A unique opportunity, yes, but a lesson to anyone struggling with the weight of other people's expectations and projections. Sometimes you just have to give the middle finger.

The semi-final was particularly stressful because I had been filming for Channel 5 until 1 am the night before. There was so much to do – as well as the live TV, there were pre-records, training and BBC Two's *It Takes Two*. I had been working every day for eleven weeks, spending a lot of time away from the kids, and it was taking its toll. I wasn't handling it very well. On top of everything, I had two dances to learn – the Argentine tango to the Eurythmics' 'Here Comes the Rain Again' and the waltz to Celine Dion's 'Only One Road'.

The choreographers said of the Argentine tango, 'If people don't think you are having an affair by the end of this then you've done it wrong.' Well, we all know how I feel about that sort of performance. On rehearsal day, less than twenty-four hours before the live semi-final, I still couldn't nail either dance even though they were relatively simple compared to what had gone before. The day of the show was hard. I couldn't get any clarity. Gorka was really stressed too. The personal fallout from the *Cabaret* dance had sent me straight back into my shell. I stopped speaking on camera and Gorka was concerned I was not coming across as myself. I knew everything I said had consequences and my priority was my kids, so I needed to make sure I didn't upset things further. I wanted to look back in ten years and still be happy with how I conducted myself. If I pulled the thread on the jumper at that point, the whole thing would unravel.

Just like the marathon running all those years previously, I started *Strictly* with something to prove to myself but it quickly became about so much more. Maybe I was there to remind people to have a go and see how far you get. Maybe I was there to give people a reminder that shit happens and you have to keep going even when you don't want to, because the world doesn't stop turning. I never mentioned the marriage break-up because I am not the first and I won't be the last. It struck a chord with many people, though, and I got a lot of messages from those having a rough time, much worse than mine. People losing children and partners to cruel illnesses, who were somehow finding a bit of a joy and light in what we were all doing on *Strictly*. What a privilege to have the opportunity to do that. I owed it to them and to myself to keep going week after week.

Will Mellor going out in the semi-finals was gutting. He brought cheek and banter. He was a geezer who spoke my language, saying things like, 'You look fit like that, go smash it, love. Your kids will be well proud.' I admit I wasn't sure I would get on with him at the beginning but he is the most loveable and loyal of characters, who knew how to say exactly the right thing at the right time. His real-life partner, Michelle McSween, is sensational, as is his dance partner, the empathetic and brilliant Nancy Xu.

Then it was the final with Hamza Yassin, Molly, Fleur and me. Gorka was emotional. I am definitely not the best dancer he's taken to the final, far from it, but I might just have been the best friend. The stress of the semi-finals was swapped for a week of joy. We had made it all the way and we had never been in a dance-off. Anything from here was the cherry on a pretty perfect cake. I am competitive and I wanted to win, but to say I would have been happy taking the trophy from any one of my fellow finalists is a lie. From week one, Hamza had sparked a fascination and an excitement in people that was insatiable. He is humble and talented, and I have no doubt he will be educating my kids in years to come. Jowita Przystał, his dance partner, is a spirit you want to be around.

Fleur is fun and classy. Her laugh is like medicine. She's survived in the industry as long as she has because she is a talent but she's deservedly loved. She has an uncanny ability to make stupid clothes look cool. Her partner Vito has a heart as big as a lion's and would probably like to own one. And Molly – well, I am probably closer in age to her mum than I am to her so I have always felt protective. I pray my daughter turns out as well as her. She partnered Carlos, a wonderful enigma on and off the dance floor.

In the week leading up to the final, heavy snow meant we had to stay in London, so I was away from Elsie for four days, the longest I had ever been away from her. I could feel myself tipping over into panic. We drove to the first day of training and passed a hill where children were sledging. A tear rolled down my cheek. Gorka said, 'Don't worry, this will be over in a few days. Remember you are a brilliant mum, but also remember you will never get this time on *Strictly* back.'

It turned out that being stuck in London was the best thing to happen because it meant we were completely immersed in final rehearsals. It took the pressure off so we could focus on the fun and enjoyment of the last few days. From week one, when I hid on the fire escape, to being in the final thirteen weeks later, I was proud and grateful. I had fought against doubt, devastation and lack of dance ability. I so loved being around the *Strictly* cast and crew and thrived on their energy and encouragement as much as I did the hard work and reward. And how lucky I was to have shared this experience with Gorka, a world-class dancer and true pal!

In preparation for the final, I was back in wardrobe with Vicky and her amazing team – this time she put a cushion under her desk in case I wanted to escape, but I didn't need it by then. We were close to Christmas and one of the wardrobe team said, 'I am shopping this weekend, do you want me to stick an extra dinosaur in?' How lovely was that? They knew I was worried about when I would have time to buy my kids' presents. They ordered food and Vicky shared it with me because she knew I wouldn't have time to eat, either. Vicky is forever the person I want to be.

On the day of the final, Mark, the set designer, stopped me, looked at me seriously and said, 'Enjoy every second, it goes so quick.' And so we did. I soaked up every smile, hug, make-up check, stitch in my gusset and stretch. I wish I could have bottled the atmosphere from that night.

As the show opened, Hamza, Molly, Fleur and I were on a platform, high above the audience. I was in my element, dancing around and being told off for moving too much. Hamza hated heights so he was very quiet. The pyrotechnics were going off around Molly's feet and she thought she would be set on fire. There was drama and excitement, and I will never forget us suspended over the show, waiting for it to start. I had conquered something big and here I was in the final with a huge smile on my face. I felt brave and it was a familiar and welcome feeling that I had not had in a long time.

We were lowered to the ground and formed a circle for the opening dance. One of the dancers, Graziano, thought it was hilarious that I had gone from being someone scared of their own shadow to the person in the middle of the circle making it up as I went along – much to Gorka's amusement. I was a woman transformed.

Gorka and I danced our jive again and a show dance to Emili Sandé's 'Shine'. Did I dance the best I ever had? Probably not, but we were happy. We saved the best for last with a repeat of *Cabaret* and scored tens across the board, ending with a top score of forty. The reaction when we finished was incredible. Craig and Motsi said that should win it. As we ran up the stairs, Tyler was at the top and he grabbed my hand and said, 'You just got a double standing ovation!' My fellow celebrities and the other dancers made us feel like we had already won. It didn't get any better than that. Claudia asked me what it would mean to win. How could I answer that truthfully?

I'll tell you now why I wanted to win – because for the last three months of leaving the house at 5am and getting home at 11pm, I had been telling my kids that Mummy was going to work to try to win a glitter ball. I had moved them from Leeds into my parents' house, where we were all sharing the back bedroom. They had left friends behind and changed schools without complaint. How to explain this to them? I used the glitter-ball trophy. My kids are sporty so they understood what getting a trophy meant. I wanted to show them how hard work conquers all. No matter what you are dealing with, you persevere and good stuff happens. I went into *Strictly* not being able to sleep and I came out of it strutting about on national TV in a corset and suspenders. I went into it having no clue how the rest of my life was going to look and I came out of it feeling like the world was my oyster.

This was the truth, but I would never have said any of that on telly. So I didn't answer honestly. Instead, I said, 'Oh it's fine, this atmosphere is better than a trophy.' Gorka looked at me in despair. I should have thanked people for sharing their lives with us and keeping us in the competition. The only thing I was determined to articulate was how grateful I was to Gorka, and that I did. He had been so invested from the beginning and had got to me this point, so I wanted to win it for him as much as for my kids. He is a credit to that show and his family. It would have been amazing to hold the glitter ball aloft, but what we had gained already was priceless. I had so many messages from people thanking me for making winning not about winning.

Hamza and Jowita are wonderful people and they deserved to win. I am pretty sure they won it in week one because watching him dance makes you smile. It's as simple as that.

I have a great photo of me after the show, still in costume, pouring glasses of champagne from a bottle my agent had sent me. There is a second photo, taken just after, with Gorka burying his head in my shoulder. We were both disappointed for a long time, but we couldn't have done any more than we did. We partied hard that night and I sang my heart out with Molly and Fleur. We threw ourselves into the celebration, and then I had to be on my radio show the following morning on a few hours' sleep.

By the end of *Strictly*, I really felt a phenomenal amount of love from everyone in the building. From the execs to runners, from hair and make-up to wardrobe, from dancers to Tess and Claudia, I really felt they all wanted me not just to survive but shine. I had wanted to end the year on a high and I did just that. I spoke to Tyler a few days later and he said it was like being on the best holiday ever with wonderful friends making memories and then it's all over. It just stops. The routine we came to rely on disappears in an instant.

I got the train back to Cumbria and a rental house I had yet to spend a single night in. My parents came to the station to collect me and brought the children with them. I thought we would go back to theirs for a night before going to the new house in the morning, but they took us straight there. Whoa, OK, no settling-in period then?! No easing me in gently?! My parents said, 'Why, what's the point? It's good for you to get straight on with your new life.' The brilliance of my parents. You crack on! They were right, as usual. Just like that, I was back to being a full-time mum and Christmas was a week away. In the final show, I had strained my groin quite badly and a couple of days later I was dragging my leg around Sports Direct trying to get Christmas presents. Back to earth with a festive bump!

There is something magical in the water at *Strictly*. My mates who had done it before had tried to tell me, but I couldn't understand until I had experienced it. It is the most amazing show in the world and yet, emotionally, it is one of the hardest things I have ever done. It may seem like just a celebrity dance show but it's a million things more than that too. It made me question everything in my life. I am not an actress or a performer, but I know Fleur felt the same way as me. It is like you are baring your soul. I went into it a wilting flower and with every week I grew stronger and happier, but it could have completely broken me.

I do have one regret, although it is not something I would change if I went back in time. *Strictly* is very real and I have made a career out of being the same, experiencing stuff and taking the audience with me. I am always conscious of the importance of that relationship. In some ways, I feel I short-changed the audience because I clammed up. I am usually too open and honest, and I say and do things I probably shouldn't because I don't have a game plan. To have your private life played out in the media is not something I would wish on my worst enemy and losing control of the narrative that you tell their kids about their lives is the most awful feeling. If I could do the show again now, as I am, maybe I would be more emotionally open and share, but at that time, I knew if I did I would fall apart and what I said could be taken out of context. Sometimes, on camera after a dance, I would just giggle because I didn't know what was safe to say.

I underestimated how much noise there was around *Strictly*. I also didn't realise how significantly it touches people's lives. I will be forever buoyed by how much the show affects people in a positive way and the way they light up when they ask me about it. I was getting the most humbling messages from people who were going through much worse things than I was and they were thanking me. One woman, whose son was terminally ill, wrote saying she watched our dances and could see in my eyes that I had to push myself out of bed and keep going. She said that on her darkest days, she saw me keeping on and she knew she had to do the same.

I still get messages now from people who ask me how I get through certain things. I don't have the answers and I am not immune to the pain. On those days when you think the couch will swallow you whole and the idea of getting up off it seems like the most impossible task, there are little things that help me, like certain songs turned up full volume, taking the day one hour at a time, getting out in the fresh air and talking things through. Sometimes you can't compute the way other people are behaving and the hardest thing can be accepting you're never going to. Over the years, I have often referred to the Japanese art of kintsugi, where gold lacquer is used to piece shards of a broken item back together, resulting in a more beautiful object once it is mended. A nice idea and a beautiful metaphor, but sometimes the vase is beyond repair and you have to let it go.

People reaching out to me reminds me I have a responsibility to keep going in case it helps others who are in a similar predicament. It's why I wanted to write this book. Among all the hundreds and hundreds of messages I received during and after *Strictly*, the ones that particularly resonated were those people who said I had shown them that it's OK to be terrified and still show up. Jayde Adams said to me, 'Do you think I feel comfortable being this size and being in a leotard and performing "Flashdance" on the telly? No I don't, but if I do it, another big lass may think, it's OK, I can wear what I want and go to the party because Jayde is.' It's so much more than just dancing.

When I did the *Strictly* tour, you wouldn't recognise me from the show. From the fire escape to London's 02, I had come a long way. It was unlikely I would ever be performing in these venues again so I lapped up every second of it. Each night on the tour, when I strode out to perform my *Cabaret* piece, the audience stamped their feet and chanted my name before the music even started. Anton said in response, 'We as performers do these gigs to get that reaction. Most of us spend our whole career waiting for that.' It was the perfect ending to my *Strictly* journey.

Strictly brought me back to life. A piece of my heart will always be sequinned.

18

The Juggle Is Real

'I had underestimated how amazing it is to watch the people who love your kids be around them regularly.'

I know I am just one of a trillion (not an official statistic) people who juggle parenting and a job. There is nothing special about my set-up. OK, so the extremes of my life can be quite intense, but the positives of my career far outweigh its negatives. I am very mindful of this every time I talk about being a working mum because I am talking from a position of privilege, considering the work I do and the family support I have. I know I am lucky to have an unconventional job that gives me flexibility and can pay well, even if I never know when or where it will end. All of that said, no matter what your background, being

253

a working parent is a constant juggle, which I can often find myself on the losing end of.

I want to have my cake and eat it too. Don't we all?! I have worked hard to get to where I am, but my priority is always my children and these two areas of my life regularly clash. I have had to make some tough decisions over the years about what I can take on and how that will impact family life. I am very protective of the time I spend with my kids because right now they need me and before I know it, they won't. I want to enjoy time with Elsie before she starts school, just like I did with the boys, so even though I would absolutely love to do everything I am offered, I say no more than I say yes. Ultimately, it isn't fair on the job, the kids or me to take on anything that sends me away for months on end. I would not be my best professional self if I was worrying about what was happening at home.

I've found having friends in the same boat as me to be a brilliant asset. Like my friends Clare and Ellen, who also do the single-parenting work juggle, and we laugh about some of the hoops we have jumped through. Clare has, on occasion, driven from Yorkshire to Cornwall and back in a day so she can go to a meeting and still see the kids. Ellen recounts the times she runs to the school gates in work boots and high vis, having navigated meetings on construction sites while being determined to do school pick-up as well.

In my twenties, I loved being away filming for big chunks of time and maybe I will feel the same way again when my kids are older. As a working parent, you always feel like there is somewhere else you are meant to be. But if you are a stay-at-home parent, you can be made to feel like you should be working. I watch friends wrestle with the fact they have given up careers they loved to be around more for their kids and support their partners. Those people deserve as much praise. Neither direction is easy. It's about owning the choices you have made, or have had to make, and doing the best you can in the circumstances. It isn't a competition between us parents to see whose life is harder and more exhausting, even though my friends and I often compare notes and make a joke out of how little sleep we get.

I know many people find this hard to believe but I don't have a childminder or a nanny; instead, I have a very busy granny! I know how lucky I am to have parents who take an active role in my children's upbringing. They are the best support system and I literally could not do it without them. I am learning how to be a good parent all the time and so much of my inspiration and guidance comes from them. They don't take over. They have found a productive way to be hands-on with the kids and also help me, which means I can still retain my independence. Mum will do little tasks like taking a parcel to the post office for me and Dad will pop in on his way to or from work. He is an additional adult voice when mine may be wavering and will say things like, 'It's not a hotel kids, you can't keep asking your mum for snacks.' Mum will look at my calendar and pre-empt situations, offering to have Elsie if she can see that I have stuff on with the boys. Them being there means I can have important one-to-one time with each of the kids. I took Ernie wakeboarding for his birthday, which he absolutely loved. I could focus on him completely while Dad took Louis to football and Mum was pottering around with Elsie at home.

If I have to work at a weekend, I worry that having all three children is a lot for my parents to take on and I will ask the local childminder if she is able to help, but Mum gets awfully put out. She thinks that I think she can't handle it. I don't think that! I just don't want her to feel that she has to be their childminder rather than their Granny. She will often ask me if it is OK if she and Dad go out for dinner with their friends, in case I need them, and I have to push them out of the door. Of course it's OK! It's their life and I would hate them to change plans or for us to monopolise their time. I know they genuinely like being here for me and the kids and I have only just learned to appreciate how much they are behind me.

As well as my parents, I have a wider support network which makes me feel emotional if I think about it for too long. I have my brother Gavin and my sister-in-law Rebecca, and they have two small boys, so the cousins spend a lot of time together. Elsie adores Gavin. Every time she sees him she puts her arms up and chases him, shouting, 'GA GA!'

He is so good with my boys too, playing football, card games and drawing with them. And then there are my best mates. I have a close-knit group of old school friends who live near each other and rely on one another. It is like an extension of family with us, in and out of each other's houses, gardens and fridges. In Leeds, we had friends but it was quite transient, so being back with my school friends is a different feeling. I had underestimated how amazing it is to watch the people who love your kids be around them regularly.

Mine have an army of 'aunties' I have known for thirty-plus years and a lot of fields and fells to play on. I hope we can support each other as adults and parents, as we did as teens. Shellie will sell things on eBay for me to help clear my mountain of chaos. Olga will entertain my boys in a way only a mother of three boys knows how. Jill is always poised with the kettle on when I randomly call by. Babs always picks up the phone, no matter what time it is and is great with sensible suggestions. Lucy lets my kids treat her house as her own and Amy's whole family is an extension of mine. When I started *Strictly,* one of my best mates, Kim, offered to have Elsie every Thursday. Initially I was reticent because I thought it was too much for her to take on. She said, 'Helen, you've got two boys I don't know because you have been away for so long. You are my best friend. I would love to build a relationship with Elsie.' And she has and it is beautiful to see. Recently, I was an hour late back from work so my friend Lucy looked after the kids until I got home. Her children and mine were playing together on the village green when I got back, so I took over from her and she went to cook dinner for her family. I am never happier than when my garden is full of my kids and other people's and I can watch muddy children kicking footballs or splashing in the paddling pool with Elsie toddling around in the middle of it all.

I really hope I haven't given the impression that my life is perfect. Far from it. There are days when I am just about keeping it all together, but I am getting better at embracing the chaos. I can be stripping the bed at midnight because the baby has been sick, or sitting in a Zoom meeting with Louis dressed as a panther on my shoulders while battling Ernie about doing homework. Sometimes I can feel as if I have done a full day before 10am and not made a good enough job of any of it.

When we lived in France, I could happily embrace motherhood without distraction because work life was almost non-existent and we spent every day on the beach or in the pool. Once I had Louis and we moved to Leeds and started all over again, I found it tricky to know where I fitted in and how my new life was going to unfurl. I looked around for clues on how to parent in this new place with two tiny children. As we made friends, I could see there was no clear path to follow. Some parents worked, some didn't. Some had nursery support or childminders, some were at home full-time. I wasn't sure what was right for us or what work I could consider. I knew I couldn't take on big challenges requiring many hours of training so the invitation to take part in *Celebrity Boxing* worked brilliantly. We made family decisions based on Richie's job, not mine, and I was happy to let that happen. I was not financially driven; my priority was being a wife and mother.

London friends can't imagine how I cope without a nanny. Cumbrian friends would think I had lost the plot if I got one. They would be like, what's wrong with us or your mam helping? On hearing my marriage was over, a TV presenter pal said to me, 'I know you are going to hate to hear this, but you are going to have to get a nanny now.' I told her I had nothing against that but it just wasn't me. Like that episode of *Motherland* where one of the characters gets a nanny who is brilliant and makes her life better but she hates it. I think that would be me. I don't need a nanny for my kids, I need a nanny for me! I want someone to put a wash on, pop a cottage pie in the oven, put all the toys away and sort out my car insurance. Those things aren't fun. Hanging out with my kids is. No judgement for whichever way people choose to organise their lives – it has to be what works for you and your family, and what is right at the moment may not be in a couple of years' time.

I know people who have employed a night nanny for their babies and adopted the practice of sleep training to make sure their children sleep through the night. None of my kids are good sleepers and they will often end up in my bed. With local friends it has become a badge of honour. How many hours of sleep have you had? Five? Oh, that's a lie-in, I've had three! It is interesting how differently people approach this. There is so much judgement around what is right and wrong when we should be doing what is good for ourselves and our family. With the advent of social media the comparisons are constant. You always think someone else is doing it better, but it's hard to know what the truth is on a beautifully curated Instagram feed. I find it is more useful to hear the realities of parenting through talking to friends of mine, particularly if they are further ahead than me and I can benefit from the mistakes they have made. I may be stressing about Ernie being rude or not sharing nicely, and a friend may say, 'Wait until you have a teenager with a new boyfriend or a vaping habit.' Every age throws up its challenges.

I know my job is difficult to understand if you aren't in the business. It is precarious at the best of times. Not only do I not know when the next job will be coming up, I also don't know when the next pay cheque will be. This sounds like a nightmare if it's not a life you are used to, but I love it because it actually gives me an element of control over what I do and when. Of course, I still miss the occasional school sports day or footie match, which hurts my heart, but there are so many important dates I can protect. The perception is that if you are busy all the time then you are a success, but being too scared to say no to stuff just makes you a busy fool. It's like, 'Oh yes, I am doing so well I am nearly at burnout!' Success to me is doing the work I want to do, balanced with a nice existence. I don't want to work seven days a week. I want to enjoy my life, which also means being at home with the kids and sitting in the garden watching them splash around in the paddling pool.

I have got better at saying no. I figure the opportunity may come around again in the future, or be presented in a different way or never, but I am OK with that. There have been times when I have struggled to make a decision. I was asked to do a breakfast radio show when Louis was tiny and we had just moved back from France. It was with people I liked and it would have been perfect. I had to turn it down because I didn't want Louis to wake up every morning without me there. I couldn't imagine not being part of his morning routine. Neither of the boys were at school at this point and I wasn't ready to give that time up. I didn't want to miss a moment. I also turned down a big entertainment show and that was incredibly hard, but I knew I could only do it if I was able to give it everything, and I wasn't. If I hadspent as much time away from my kids as

I would have needed to to do that job, it would have madee me really unhappy and affected my professionalism, which would mean I would not be the best version of myself. I feel the same about travel programmes. I love them and they were a big part of my early career, but I have had to shelve anything too far away or longer term because of the logistics of travel and the potential for overrun. I couldn't risk not being able to get home because it's just me. It would impact too heavily on the kids and the people who are helping me out.

Maybe our work focus improves once we have children because we don't have time to waste on the politics of the place, pointless meetings or ineffective practices. Being a mum has made me more efficient and empathetic at times. I am also clear about when I am available, as we have all become too contactable and once a message is sent the expectation is that it will be read immediately. It's doubly hard when you are freelance in a competitive industry, so a slow response could be costly, but I don't think this approach does anything for our mental health. If I am with the kids I want to be fully engaged with what they are doing, not standing to the side with my face stuck in a screen or the phone wedged to my ear. If they are jumping in the lake I want to be jumping in with them, not responding to emails as soon as they ping in. We need to be protective of our boundaries because nobody else will be.

Recently, I had to have a difficult conversation with my

boss, Heidi Dawson, controller of BBC Radio 5 Live and 5 Sports Extra. I have known Heidi since we worked together on *Newsround* and our paths crossed again recently when I joined Radio 5 to host their Sunday morning show. This was something I had been working towards for years. It was a dream job and as soon as I started, I knew I was in the right place. But when everything changed in my personal life I had to seriously rethink my weekly schedule and whether working every Sunday morning was feasible. The truth was, it wasn't. Both my boys have sport clubs and matches at the weekend and I couldn't bear the idea that they wouldn't have a parent cheering them on from the sidelines. Of course, my family and friends would have pitched in but there are certain times when only Mum or Dad will do and this was one of them. When Richie and I were together it worked really well because I would be at home all week and then go to work on Sunday and he would take the boys to rugby. I thought I had found the perfect solution so to have to extricate myself made me feel sick.

Not only had I worked hard to get the gig, but so had my agent, the production company and Heidi. Everyone had pulled it off and given me my heart's desire and now I had to tell them all I couldn't do it. My stomach was in a knot when I walked into Heidi's office but I knew I needed to speak to her woman to woman, mother to mother. It was a difficult conversation for me to broach, but it was productive. We had known each other a long time and I really didn't want to let her down. Heidi has two children so she completely understood, which made it so much easier to talk to her. She appreciated my honesty and said there was no point in us trying to do something that was not sustainable. What a breath of fresh air! She knew I couldn't be good at my job if I didn't have a happy life. How could I interview people if I wasn't part of the real world? Turning up at the school gate, looking after my own children and experiencing the daily grind makes me a better mum and broadcaster.

These days we are expected to have it all, but how?! As we fill our houses with appliances designed to make life easier the pressure to be perfect just keeps piling on. It's impossible for many families to live on one salary, which means both parents are working and trying to do the best they can with the time they have. We are all looking for balance. I used to take the kids to about seventy-five (slight exaggeration to illustrate the point) activities every week. It was exhausting and I wondered if they really wanted to do them all or was I taking them because I would feel like a bad mum if I didn't? I want them to have as many opportunities as possible, but this can easily tip into too many.

It makes me laugh when people ask how I juggle everything, as if I may have the answers. I don't, although my lawyer friend Jill is incredibly practical and has given me lots of tips that I live by. In case it is helpful, I have put together a list of my 'life hacks' – if you can even call them such a thing. Please feel free to skip to the next chapter if you are the sort of uber-organised person who is never without matching socks. If not, check out the below. Seeing it written down makes me realise I am not quite as chaotic as I think I am, although my family and friends may have something to say about that . . .

Get a cleaner if you can afford to

This was the first piece of advice Jill gave me. Weirdly, I didn't do this when I was married because I thought cleaning was part of my role as a wife. I know! I've abandoned that ideal, but I'm aware it is a huge privilege to have a lovely lady who comes around a couple of times a week to clean the house, change the bedsheets and help me keep on top of domestic stuff. Coming home to a clean and tidy house is like an injection of sunshine.

Organise a milk delivery

Again, thanks for this suggestion goes to Jill, who pointed out that if I ran out of milk I would not be able to leave the children and nip to the shops. I live in a rural village and there is no Deliveroo, but the milkman can bring a number of items which really helps me out.

Embrace batch-cooking

I hate cooking; it's a total chore. So when I do it, I really go for it. I make double helpings and freeze them. There is a woman in our village who does home catering and she will make a lasagne or a big pot of chilli and deliver to the doorstep. It's a lovely home-cooked luxury. And I always have fish fingers in the freezer ready to save the day.

Have a present drawer

As in a place to put gifts ready for children's friends' birthdays. I may forget the wrapping paper and card, but there is always an age-appropriate treat ready to go. Believe me, with two children at primary school and one at nursery, there are a lot of parties.

Share lifts

I share lifts with another mum for sport clubs and matches, so we take it in turns to ferry the kids around. It means every other week I have a slightly easier schedule, which benefits Elsie too.

Get uniforms prepped

You may find this hard to believe but on a Friday night I get the uniforms organised ready for Monday. I roll up socks, pants, shorts and top into a little package. I hate that Monday morning feeling and the panic that comes with the search for lost school shoes. Monday Me always thanks Friday Me for being organised.

Get a wipe board

Oh, how I adore my wipe board! It runs from Monday to Sunday and it's an absolute godsend. I am likely to forget my own name on busy weeks so this is where I write everything down, even the things that are the same every week. On a Sunday night I love wiping the board clean and starting again – small pleasures! It also means Mum can refer to it. She is super-organised so this approach really appeals to her and it makes me look like I am in control.

Think about your bedsidemanner

I have swapped my phone for an alarm clock so I no longer need it next to my bed. If the kids fall asleep on me I end up scrolling through my phone looking at clothes I don't even like, which is not a good use of my time. I also have a notebook by my bed because invariably I will wake up in the middle of the night remembering things I had forgotten I had to do. I make a note of it and add it to a never-ending list. It helps me get back to sleep because I feel like I have emptied my head.

Take time out

I don't get much of this. Even clothes shopping is for work, not for pleasure. As for a social life, I have to prioritise work events, so I don't get to do as much with my friends as I would like to. Big nights out at restaurants, clubs and bars don't interest me as much anymore. There is nothing better than sitting around a friend's kitchen table with a large glass of wine and a big bowl of crisps, putting the world to rights.

Pack a bag

I keep the kids' swimming bags in the boot of the car so we can be as flexible as possible. In the winter, it is handy if we decide to go to the leisure centre after school. In the summer, it means everythingis ready for an impromptu visit to the lake. So I have a bag with swimmers, wetsuits, shoes and towels ready to go. I also have food in the fridge that can be transformed into a picnic so we can eat wherever we go. I buzz off the summer and lighter nights so I don't want to miss a minute of sun.

Lower your expectations

There are some parts of parenting where I try and make it easy on myself. There is always something that won't be done, or expertly achieved, because I am splitting myself in three. Another reason to limit the after-school activities. I pick and choose what I can delegate, but there are tasks I wouldn't hand over because they feel like parenting rites of passage. Like doing the party food for the children's birthdays.

Go with the flow

This is a bit like my point above but more to do with social time with the kids. I try not to get stressed about the little things and am better at being relaxed about bedtime. I love hanging out with my kids. I set boundaries but I don't want to be constantly battling them either. So if bathtime is late, that's OK. And if they go into school with dirty knees then that's OK too.

Treasure your friends

I have friends from different walks of life who can bring a new perspective. I know I have people who are there for me no matter what, but I also know I need to invest in those friendships. I have talked a lot about my home friends, but my Leeds girls were an army of support when I needed it most. That support can carry you through testing times. The friends who turn up and read one of your children a bedtime story as you put the others to bed. The friends who bring you fruit and make you a sandwich in the middle of the day. The friends who take the dog out for you if it's raining. The friends who move pieces of furniture for you. You need friends the older you get, and if you're lucky enough to have good ones then treasure them.

Family grounding

My family won't ever let me feel sorry for myself or play the victim. I have the kind of parents who come out with one-liners that are annoyingly bang-on. It's like they coined Instagram quotes before Instagram quotes were a thing. 'Worry about what you don't have and you'll waste what you do have' and 'There's always someone worse off than yourself' are two of their favourites! Maybe it's their personalities or maybe it's their upbringing, but their matter-of-fact attitude keeps me grounded.

19

Fabulous at Forty

*'My children show me how to find the joy,
hope and fun in every day.'*

My house is often mayhem. It's three against one in the child-to-adult ratio and they are a spirited bunch. Tempers flare, nappies explode, baked beans are spilled and toys are thrown. The age gap between my youngest and eldest means that the drama can range from the baby scaling the stairs and emptying drawers to doors slamming and arguments over Nerf guns. Until recently, we had a dog too. A beautiful and stupid Labrador called Spiderman who could unravel a toilet roll in seconds and cover a freshly made bed in muddy pawprints. I had to admit it was too much for me to manage and not fair on him, so he is living with my friend Helena, who loves him like a child. I miss him so much but I know he is happy and four against one is a step too far at the moment.

Ernie, my eldest, is really good at reading a situation. He will stand back and observe things before making astute, emotionally smart comments that catch me off-guard and make my heart burst. Like me, he wants to be doing something or going somewhere all the time. I can be putting Elsie to bed and asking the boys to get into their pyjamas and turn around to find him back in the paddling pool. He ekes out every single minute of the day. The wind-down for bed can often involve him asking for one final bike ride around the village and I find that impossible to resist. He is so confident and curious; you never know where the day is going to end with Ernie. I love that he is growing into his personality and he is such good company. When I took him wakeboarding for his birthday he was thrilled, and I was in heaven doing it with him. We share a daredevil spirit and a sociable gene. He won't have a party with just a few friends if he can put a bouncy castle on the village green and invite everyone. And nobody bats an eyelid when he puts out his birthday candles with a water pistol. When he was a toddler, we were in the park one day and before I knew it, he had invited himself on to a woman's mobility scooter and she was taking him for a jaunt around the park. Some say he is 'spirited' and I say, 'You're welcome!' That's my Ernie.

As for Louis, my middle child, there isn't a person I know who isn't charmed by him. He is so funny. I know I am biased but he is also super cute with big Bambi eyes. He calls himself 'Koala Baby' because he loves climbing inside my jumper and clinging on to me. While Ernie can be a bit of a firecracker and go off at any time, Louis is much more laidback; we called him 'zen baby' when he first arrived. That doesn't mean he doesn't get angry, and he can be incredibly blunt – he says it like it is. He also loves a chat and is much more relaxed in a grown-up environment than walking into a room full of kids he doesn't know. In the school holidays, Ernie will want to sign up to every sports camp but Louis will ask to come to work with me, and I can take him anywhere. He always has lots of questions. He is a total crowd-pleaser. I took him to a voice-over job and he sat under the desk playing with cards for so long that the engineer said, 'I thought he had gone, he was so quiet.' While Ernie is a natural sportsman, Louis has to try harder, but I think this will serve him well in the long run. They could both play football and cricket all day.

It's harder to pinpoint who Elsie will become because she is still a toddler, but she is exactly like Ernie was. She is always on the go, fiercely independent and never stops. Her tenacity, strength and confidence overflow already so goodness knows what she will be like by the time she starts school! At playgroup, she will climb the furniture around the room rather than play with the toys. Her nursery teacher said she could tell Elsie has older brothers because she's pretty feisty. She will be in the paddling pool surrounded by boys who will splash and shoot her with water pistols and she just roars with laughter. There is no fear and no tears.

She is a restless sleeper, so when she wakes up in the morning she has this unruly mass of curls which makes her look like a mad professor. Recently, I was at football with the boys, with Ernie playing on one pitch and Louis on the other and Elsie freewheeling between the two. My old high-school boyfriend rocked up with his daughter, who is the same age as Elsie, and he asked where she was. I pointed over to Elsie, who was on the other side of the football pitch, arms outstretched to one of the parents to pick her up. She was missing a shoe, there was chocolate all down her front and she was holding a sweet. By comparison, his daughter was spotless in white with hair slides in her neatly brushed hair, sitting in a very clean pushchair. As he walked off, my friend said, 'Well, Helen, there are two girls who are never going to play together!'

My kids can't leave a room without jumping over a piece of furniture. Why walk when you can run or parkour your way about instead, clambering over everything in your path?! They will assess anything in an attempt to climb it. Elsie loves nothing more than running around in circles. After school and at the weekend, they want to set off on their bikes for an adventure or be on a football or cricket pitch. Water plays a big part in their lives, as it has in mine, so the paddling pool is up from Easter and we go to the river or lake every week. While other children are crying about the cold and the fish, mine strip off and get straight in. We were in London a while ago and I took them to some of the touristy children's attractions. At the end of the trip, I asked them what they loved most and to mark the experiences out of ten. They gave Hamleys and KidZania a jolly seven. They gave the park in Shepherd's Bush a big fat ten because they spent the entire time running around and climbing on everything. I think that says it all. We live where we do because it is good for us all.

I can't imagine the four of us living in Leeds now and I am not sure how long my kids would have lasted in the city anyway. Before we moved back to Cumbria, we would visit regularly and it was hard to head back to the city. Before I had kids, I had an expectation of what sort of mother I would be and the type of children I would have, which makes me laugh out loud now. One of my assumptions was that it would be important for them to do well at school and my job would be to nurture their academic abilities. Now I have them, all I want is for them to be happy, confident and have lovely friends. I don't believe kids are as resilient as we think they are – they need love, support and laughter. So many children struggle with anxiety. It's been a difficult time for kids post-Covid, and with the constant seduction of screens and the internet. Mine are no different, but I work hard to get them outside and I try to find things in the natural world which will excite them. I had an idyllic upbringing but I didn't appreciate it at the time, so seeing my kids do the things I did, like enjoying long bike rides down country lanes and spending light evenings by the lake, gives me so much joy.

Ernie, Louis and Elsie are so lucky to have each other and I am sure as hell lucky to have them. They have always been my reason for getting out of bed in the morning, for keeping fit and eating healthily, because I want to be on this planet long enough to see them grow up. I go to work so I can buy them the football boots they want. They show me how to find the joy, hope and fun in every day. Having children never clipped my wings or stopped me taking on adventures – it's crafted new and different ones.

Is it hard, without the traditional set-up and them waking up to their two parents in the same house? Of course. There will always be moments, occasions that aren't easy, but that is life. There are so many people who have been in my position without the opportunities I have, so I hope sharing a little of my experience may help others not feel so alone, or like you did something wrong. You didn't. And it will be OK. Maybe better than OK.

I think when you have shared a life with someone and been

part of each other's highs, lows, break-downs and build-backs, it can be difficult to move on. When you see people whose dreams and plans you shared doing things and acting in a way that you can't get your head around it can be difficult to compute. I don't think that makes a person mad, or toxic, or bitter. I think that makes a person human. Feel your feelings. If you are grieving your relationship, if the end caught you by surprise, it's OK to be sad. But you have to keep putting one foot in front of the other. Keep feeling the grass between your toes. Keep being around people who make you laugh. Keep listening to Taylor Swift and Kelly Clarkson and know it is going to be OK. Keep a few people in your phone who you trust and can call anytime to vent and offload. I offloaded so much at one point I think my friends were actually feeling more hurt than me, and ironically that's when I gave myself a kick up the arse. You can't drag other people down with you and so at some point, you have to draw a line in the sand, for you and the people around you.

I spoke to a friend whose partner had recently left him and I recommended a babysitter and someone who might drop off home-made meals. He told me weeks later that it was the first time he'd had a conversation as if it was all going to be OK. I hadn't asked how he was. I'dsaid, 'I know you're not OK but I know you will be because you have children and parents, so you don't have to think about next week or next year, just the next hour.'

I grew up with two parents who loved each other and still do, over forty years on, and who put their kids first. I know how valuable this is and how rare. This is my reference point and it is what I wanted for my own family, the fairy tale I suppose. I haven't deleted my old Instagram posts because they reflect how things were at the time. I don't want to rewrite the narrative of our past. I want Richie to be in our children's lives as much as possible and I want them to know that we loved each other, but things change and that's OK too.

I know there will be moments ahead which will hurt but I am so excited for what is to come. By this I do not mean a boyfriend. The amount of people who have said to me, 'Oh, don't worry, you will find someone else!' Why would I want someone else to work my life around?! I want to enjoy this time of focusing on my kids and my career; I don't need to try to find energy I don't have for a new relationship. When I was on *Strictly* one of the male dancers said, 'I can't wait to see who you date next!' Which was very sweet of him, but I said, 'What are you talking about? I am a forty-year-old divorced mother of three!' And he said, 'Exactly! Isn't that wonderful? You have got your career, your family and your house. You know what you are about. You don't NEED a man, you just want one.' I could see what he was trying to say.

There can be silver linings to tough situations if you look hard enough, and one of my shiniest rewards has been moving back to Cumbria. Since I have come home it proves to me it takes a village and I have that, metaphorically and actually. Some of my neighbours are people I have grown up with and friends of my parents – I can't step outside my front gate without saying hello to someone I know. It's lovely and it also takes some getting used to. When I first moved in, a neighbour I didn't know came up to me and said he had heard how well the boys were settling in at school. At first it really threw me. Then I worked out he was a friend of my parents and used to be a governor at the school. My mindset shifted from 'Who on earth are you?!' to 'How lovely that people are looking out for my kids'.

I am waiting for the novelty to wear off and make me pine for the anonymous city, but it hasn't yet. We have a good word-of-mouth network and a village WhatsApp. When I lost my AirPods out walking in the village, someone found them and dropped them around the following day. I am not sure that would have happened in a lot of places. Maybe I came back here out of necessity, the familiarity of friends and family, maybe it's as simple as childcare support, but you can't deny the romance. The fells. The fields. The country pubs and quaint villages. I am getting older and I am ready for it.

Of course, there are quirks that can land with a sting. A neighbour asked me why my car was back so late. Another pointed out the registration of a friend's car who had visited.

My friend Jill, who had been on a very intense work trip to Barcelona, was greeted by a similar neighbour with 'How was your holiday, nice time?' as she arrived back to wrestle her three small children. It's that kind of well-meaning mentality that could get claustrophobic, but the pros outweigh the cons.

It is also priceless to me that my parents, brother and sister-in-law know all of my kids' best friends, and football and cricket coaches. I love being back in the bosom of my large extended family too. I am from the kind of family where we have a big WhatsApp group of aunts, uncles and cousins, so I know when my auntie is doing her hoovering or grocery shopping, or when my cousins' kids are in school plays. There is a real security in that sort of solid network of incredible people who love me and whom I love. I grew up in this community and it has given me a wonderful identity and assurance. It has fared me well.

I had the most nationally humiliating year but I am not embarrassed. I know I can't control everything; all I can control is my reaction to what happens to me. Am I strong and stoic? Nope, I am just getting on with it. The clock ticks and there is only so much time to wallow because there are many people in really difficult situations. I think this reaction is rooted in where I am from. I am accountable to the people around me. Actions have consequences and there is no hiding from that. I was brought up in the kind of place where, if you do something naughty, it reflects badly on your family and the wider community. Everyone knows about it very quickly. I don't think that is a bad way to grow up. The last thing I would want is to upset my family and I hope I can instil the same respect in my kids. We talk about apologising if you have done something you shouldn't and I will make them say it to the person and even write a card. They find it mortifying and that's the point. It's not a nice feeling but it's important to own your behaviour and be able to say sorry – we all make mistakes but in a world where everyone seems to blame everyone else I think it's important to be able to say, 'I messed up. I need to have a word with myself and make sure I don't do that again.' Accountability is important to me. Own it and apologise. Shit happens; we don't have to make other people feel shitty in the process.

I am a big fan of 'sticking your head in' – by which I mean, popping in to see someone without warning or receiving visitors without inviting them. I didn't realise that this sort of behaviour doesn't happen everywhere. My London friends used to think it was odd that I would just call around for a cup of tea. Apparently, it's rude to just turn up when you are passing without being asked to or withoutcalling ahead to signal your intention! I am a really sociable person, which is probably another way of saying I don't like to spend too much time on my own. One of my pals, Eric, lives in west London and he comes from a farming community like me. He has managed to create this little network of friends who think nothing of calling on each other, so I would 'stick my head' in to see him and we would raise eyebrows at how formal city folk were.

I hate that I am making such stereotypical assumptions but I thought about it a lot recently when I filmed with my friend Dan Walker. We made a series for Channel 5 in which we travelled up and down the Pennines. We made four episodes celebrating the Pennines, people and places. Dan couldn't believe how many people I knew and in how many shops I found people who knew my parents or I had mutual connections with. I like people. It's who I am and I will always give you the warmth you give me. One day, we went to a village and had afternoon tea with a knitting circle, and Dan was totally charmed by it. It was delightful but it wasn't unusual to me, it's just life, but his reaction made me remember how special this is. I know not everyone can live in a rural village where people have time to knit in a circle – but don't underestimate the power of community wherever you are, be that gym friends, work friends or mates you meet at the school gates.

I never take the landscape of my home for granted. Recently, I was on a FaceTime with Tyler and Molly, my mates from *Strictly,* and Tyler spotted the field behind me full of sheep. He said, 'Is that a field behind you? With actual sheep in?' Erm, yes. It's all there is around here. It reminded me how many people don't have access to rural spaces. Some people are so far removed from the countryside that they wouldn't know how to enjoy it or have the confidence to walk around in it. It's one of the reasons why I love working on programmes like *This Week on the Farm* because it brings rural life into people's sitting rooms. The audience figures continue to grow, which proves how drawn to it people are.

When I was a child, Mum would say in a dreamy voice, 'Oh, look at the fells' and I would think, *And . . . ?* Now I am a mum, I say the same to my three all the time. I want them to understand how fortunate they are to live where they do, so I always point out the view, the weather and things of interest. I hope it will get under their skins, like it did mine. I feel rooted to this beautiful place. I try to get out in it as much as possible, with and without the kids. I even schedule work calls so I can walk and talk, or arrange to catch up with a friend while we hike. My head works better in fresh air and my soul feels better immersed in greenery. I am not a fair-weather walker either. As I write this, I have just come off a rain-soaked fell. With the rain and wind in my face and my legs burning, every bit of me felt alive and for that time, all I thought about was where I was. If bad weather can be handled safely, it often makes for a more satisfying adventure.

*   *   *

I will always give credit where it is due and yet never to myself. So this is another reason why I wanted to write this book, to remind myself of all the good things in my past and how far I have come. I am not defined by a rough couple of years because I have had four amazing decades. I was genuinely excited about turning forty because it felt like a line in the sand. I can't flick a switch and pretend I am happy about the things I didn't want to happen, but growing older means we have to adapt – in the same way we have to accept hangovers take days to get over, and glasses are needed for the laptop now. I am older, seasoned in love and loss, and that just makes forty seem so much more enjoyable. I don't have a choice but if I could choose experience and being battle-ready over naïvety, I would take the former. So here's to forty. There are so many women in their fifties, sixties and seventies who have proudly lived their lives with war wounds, tales of mischief and mistakes. They have important stories to share. I want to sit with those women and listen. For me, that's what getting older is about. Maybe I am finally earning a seat at the grown-ups table.

I told Mum there was a discussion about a girl's trip to Ibiza for my birthday but I didn't think I should go. She told me not to be so ridiculous. 'It's a blink of an eye between forty and sixty,' she said, 'you have to go.' Then she reminisced about her fortieth and all of us cycling down to the pub for a lager and a packet of crisps. Not quite as glamorous. When I told her someone had called me a feminist, she said, 'Oh, bless you,' like it was a bad thing. I said, 'Mum, it's a compliment!' I remember suggesting to her 'me time' might be good. She said there was no such thing in her day, but she did think I needed to keep a smile on my face and patience for what can seem like endless days and nights with three children.

None of us know what is in our future, there is no certainty, but I feel such hope and excitement. If my kids are happy then I am happy. I can't wait to see what they do and what each stage brings, but I also hate the feeling of them slipping through my fingers. I want to slow time and prolong each stage for fear that I will turn around and they will all have left home. I dread that.

I hope I can take all the lessons I have learned so far and use them to make good choices in the future, but I also know I am capable of making a bad decision and that's OK. That's life. That's what makes us human, and in my job, I think that's what makes me able to talk to people. I hope I have empathy and kindness; they are vital qualities to me. It is important to be happy and live life, but I will never do so at someone else's expense. One analogy that has served me well is to imagine my backyard and not to let anything in it that will cause drama and stress. Equally, don't go into anyone else's backyard and cause drama and stress. Simple but effective.

I have leaned heavily on family and friends so all my gratitude goes to them, especially my parents. At some point, they will need me and I want to repay the love and support they have given me and mine. It is yet another thing that anchors me to home. Returning to the place I am from, surrounded by the people I love and the familiarity of the natural world, has been the best tonic.

At the beginning of the book, I asked how we find confidence, resilience and courage, and I hope the stories throughout have gone some way towards answering this. For me, the secret is to step into the great outdoors or unknown territory and challenge myself. The knowledge that I can do difficult things acts as a benchmark and a talisman for the way I live my life. There have been many times when I have been at physical and emotional rock bottom and I have wanted to bail from the challenge I have been presented with. When I have been close to the point where wild horses would not have been able to drag me to continue moving forward. But I have known that if I persevere I will get there. If I can do hard things, so can you because, believe me, the rewards are worth it.

You don't need to take this to some of the extreme lengths I did. Sometimes the smallest moments can be impactful too. I can feel euphoric after pushing Elsie in her pram across the fields for a couple of hours. I always think being outside gives the same buzz you get from the day after a terrible hangover when you wake up and everything looks bright and possible again. Using my body, whether it's a daily walk or pushing it to its limits, is a way to quieten my mind. It stops me overthinking and brings me immediately into the moment. When I take on a challenge, I don't think about the bigger picture, I just concentrate on the next hour and then the one after that. You just have to get on with it. Everything is doable if you think about it bit by bit, one foot in front of the other on a journey back to ourselves.

Thank you for coming with me on this trip through the magical, heart-pounding and occasionally amusing adventures that have shaped the person I am today. I hope at the very least you have been entertained and maybe even inspired at times. Here I am, grateful to be entering my fifth decade, with my three best little pals. I know there will be bumps in the road, but I also know the secret to surviving them . . . just keep going.

Acknowledgements

This is the part where I get to thank all the brilliant people who helped make this book a reality and mention those who have been glorious guardian angels at different times of my life.

Firstly, my indebted gratitude to the team at Headline Publishing including my mighty editor Yvonne Jacob, Raiyah Butt and Lucy Brazier, as well as Liz Marvin, Rosie Margesson and Vicky Beddow. Thanks also to Caroline Young and Sophie Ellis for the fab cover design. You all made this process so much easier and more enjoyable than I ever imagined. There wouldn't be a book without you (literally).

To my management team at YMU, Nick Worsley, Amber

Acknowledgements

Scott, and Anna Dixon, thank you for your hard work and for always humouring me. Thank you to my long-suffering agent and friend, Emma Rigarlsford, who listens to me, laughs with me, knows my priorities, doesn't yell at me because I can't use Google calendar, has the conversations I don't want to have, reminds me of my worth and looks better than anyone should in golf gear. Love you long time Riggles! The same appreciation to Gaby Levy and Max Dundas from Dundas PR, for steering the ship and for always going above and beyond.

Thank you to Paul Teague, my first boss at Radio Cumbria, who encouraged me to audition for *Newsround* which set my telly career wheels in motion. And to John Hawkins, Susanna Boccaccio, Livvy Ellis and all the gang at Border Television who got me excited about television and how it's made.

Forever grateful to Sinead Rocks, Simon Goretzki and Ronan Breen at *Sportsround* and *Newsround* who gave me the best grounding in the business, made it look seem like fun and showed me where to get a drink or five after work. And to Tim Levell, who took me to *Blue Peter* and subsequently sent me on a world of adventures with the best people, presenters Ayo Akinwolere, Joel Defries, Barney Harwood and Lindsay Russel. And Dawn Langan, Eric McFarland, Gav Barclay and Kieron Schiff, who were just some of the fabulous *Blue Peter* producers who I crossed the globe with.

To Stephen Cook and Michael Jackson, who gave me

opportunities and great times in sport after my days at *Blue Peter* and Steve Rudge, who let me wield a microphone around at Wimbledon. Thanks guys!

Thank you, to editor, Jo Brame, for letting me join the *Countryfile* gang. And to my fellow presenters, Adam Henson, Charlotte Smith and Matt Baker, for the many laughs and discussions over the years.

To producer Paul Stead, who has backed, humoured and harboured me more times than I care to remember. Technically my boss, but really my friend. His loyalty knows no bounds. *This Week on the Farm* is a joy to be a part of, which is also due to Rob, Dave and the wider Nicholson clan, as well as Jules Hudson and JB Gill. We are all a family on that show. We laugh a lot. Too much, you could say.

Many thanks also goes to Laura Caveney at ITV for always giving me chances and the same to BBC 5 Live's Heidi Dawson, Richard Maddox and Ben Frow.

Huge appreciation to all the *Strictly* team, especially Stefania Aleksander, for giving me a shot on the show and Gorka Marquez and Kai Widdrington, for quite literally holding my hand and repeatedly hoisting me in the air. To Lisa Davey, for making me sit in the make-up chair for more than ten minutes which consequently meant I looked OK on telly and the *Strictly* girls, for showing me what sass and 'owning it' really means.

Thank you to my first agent, Joanna Kaye and writer/

broadcaster, Emma Freud for introducing me to the wonder that is Comic Relief and for being cool women.

OK, pass the tissues for this next bit. To my parents, Richard and Janet Skelton, the goodest of good people who taught me to laugh instead of cry and to just crack on. Saying thank you is never going to be enough. And to my brother, Gavin, sister-in-law, Rebecca and my nephews who keep me grounded and Maureen for reminding me what compassion and forgiveness is and explaining 'no' is a full sentence. Everlasting thanks to my girls for making me laugh, answering my calls, feeding my children and being my dear friends, and thanks to my cousins, for being the sisters I need.

Finally, to Ernie, Louis and Elsie . . . the reason for it all.

Picture Credits

1, all) Courtesy of the author

2, all) Courtesy of the author

3, all) BBC Archive

4, top) Comic Relief/Getty Images

4, below left and right) Courtesy of the author

5, all) Courtesy of the author

6, top left) Courtesy of the author

6, middle right) Brian Sokol/Comic Relief/Getty Images

6, middle left and below right) Sean Dempsey/PA Images/Alamy

7, top left and middle right) Mike Carling/Comic Relief/Getty Images

7, middle left) Mike Egerton/PA Images/Alamy

7, below right) Courtesy of the author

8, all) Courtesy of the author

Picture Credits

9, top left and top right) James Flood/Comic Relief/Getty Images

9, middle left) Pete Dadds/Channel 4

9, below left) Courtesy of the author

10, all) Courtesy of the author

11, top) Courtesy of the author

11, middle) Steven Paston/PA Images/Alamy

11, below) Steve Flynn/News Images/Alamy

12, top left and right) Courtesy of author

12, below) Guy Levy/BBC Archive

13, all) Courtesy of author

14, top left, top right) Courtesy of author

14, below) Shutterstock

15, top right) Shutterstock

15, middle and below right) Courtesy of author

16, all) Courtesy of author